MW00453443

BREATHWORK
DETOX

HOW to THRIVE
IN THE AGE OF ANXIETY

THE
ALL-IN-ONE
PHYSICAL,
MENTAL AND
EMOTIONAL
DETOX

From the #1 Bestselling Author of *The World Is Yours...*
KURTIS LEE THOMAS

DISCLAIMER:

The Content and information provided in this book are intended for informational purposes only. No claims are made by Kurtis Lee Thomas as to specific health benefits and are NOT considered to be any prescriptions or healthcare information whatsoever. Information provided in this book is NOT intended to diagnose, mitigate, treat or cure any disease or condition whatsoever. Individuals should consult with their doctor or a qualified health care provider for medical advice. The user assumes all responsibility and risk for the use of the information in this book. THE CONTENT IN THIS BOOK HAS NOT BEEN EVALUATED OR APPROVED BY THE FDA. KURTIS LEE THOMAS RELINQUISHES ALL RESPONSIBILITY AND LIABILITY ASSOCIATED WITH ANY INFORMATION, SERVICES OBTAINED, OR PRACTICES BASED ON THE CONTENTS IN THIS BOOK.

BLASTOFF

BLASTOFF Publishing
825 Wilshire Blvd #117
Santa Monica, CA 90401

TABLE OF CONTENTS

Chapter 24

Chapter 25

Chapter 26

Resources

FOREWORD BY TIBERIUS GRANDE, FOUNDER OF LAW OF ATTRACTION LIVE

We live in a golden age of potential and possibility, an age where the average person has access to more information, more resources, and more options than ever before. We can achieve anything we want more quickly and elegantly, because technology is abundant and information flows freely with new opportunities arising every day.

Yet with all the books, seminars, lecturers, principles, and theoretical tools, we find many people still struggling, feeling stuck, exhausted, anxious, and overwhelmed, more than ever.

I was born into communism and suffered mental, physical, and emotional abuse. When the system was dismantled, we suffered oppression, poverty, and lack. Within the first two years of my life, my parents had a messy divorce. I spent the next seven years in some of the worst hospitals in the world, where malpractice was the norm. I was scarred by a third-degree burn and had multiple surgeries to correct a congenital disability. We had no way to fight or correct the system, and the communist system encouraged beatings and fear-induced punishments to keep children in their proper place.

Insecurity, lack of self-confidence, timidity, anxiety, and depression were my partners throughout my childhood and early life. At the same time, as a child, I also received love. As bad as things were, my mother and grandmother told me that they loved me and that I was an amazing child. My stepfather worked day and night at times to provide for the family. Times were still tough; sometimes all the anger and frustration were taken out on me and my sister, but we were loved.

One day when I was 19, I watched the movie *The Secret*. That movie gave me hope. If I could just read, learn, and do everything possible, I would succeed and overcome my adversity. If I dream big and do my part, the Universe will work its magic and meet me halfway.

I went on to create the Law of Attraction LIVE platform which attracted a community of manifesters over two million and growing. This led me on an amazing journey of self-discovery and material success: being able to become financially independent, working with some of the most influential speakers in the world, becoming certified to help other people, and growing online communities with millions of followers that inspire and connect people from around the world.

However, the pain was still there from the trauma and abuse my inner child suffered. He couldn't be himself, be free, or be understood. No matter how much I learned and grew as an individual the pain was still there like a splinter in my mind which I learned to live with. As I was becoming more successful on the material plane, I felt my shadow past becoming stronger and stronger. The tools I had such as visualizing, affirmations, and expressing gratitude were becoming more and more inefficient.

One day, the Universe delivered another blessing to me... the blessing of BREATHWORK. In 2012, I had the "luck" of meeting two incredibly talented ladies who rented a yoga room in our center in Bucharest, Romania. They were hosting a holotropic breathwork class under the philosophy and scientific studies of Stanislav Grof. Even though I wasn't trained in this style of spiritual and personal development, I enthusiastically joined the session. It involved a breathwork practice coupled by 2-3 hours of intense music. The theory was that we could tap into the infinite power of our subconscious mind and allow it to emerge and to heal us. I was skeptical, to say the least, but I gave my usual 100% effort.

Those three hours provided more perspective, healing, past reconciliation, and freedom than hundreds of books and the many tens of thousands of dollars I had invested in success conferences until that moment. I went on an inner journey where I trusted and allowed my subconscious to do its work and heal me. I went deep into the wounds of my childhood and healed them. I sat with that little child and loved him, hugged him, told him it's okay to make mistakes and no matter what he does he will always be loved and never punished. To my surprise, the child told me something too that changed my world forever; the little me said: "Please understand I am a child and whatever happened to me, I am happy! Now go and live your life happily and never be concerned about me... I am happy."

Words cannot describe what that experience did for me, my soul, my emotions, and my freedom as a human being. That is just the tip of the iceberg. I did many sessions after that, and many ceremonies, which led to me developing a daily breathwork practice.

The teacher, the master, the healer, the manifester, and "the way" are inside you. The books we read, the podcasts we listen to, and the conferences we attend are nothing in comparison to the infinite wisdom and potential of our sub-conscious mind, which represents 95% of who we are and how we behave. Breathwork helps us access this power and rewrite our own story.

The new era in personal development is to create change from the inside out and make ourselves our most excel-lent teacher by trusting ourselves, trusting our bodies, trusting our emotions, and working with guides to help us go within.

This is where Kurtis comes along to assist you. Trust the process, trust his guidance, and let him take you on a jour-ney within! Magic will start happening, and your life will progressively unfold into something more wonderful and majestic.

Our community is extremely grateful and happy for the new wave of growth, awakening, and enlightened living that is happening in the personal development space.

Enjoy the journey you are about to embark on while reading this book and thank you Kurtis for sharing your gift with the world.

—Tiberius Grande, Founder of Law Of Attraction LIVE, Therapist & Trainer

THE BREATHWORK INTRODUCTION
YOU SHOULDN'T SKIP

When's the last time you thought of oxygen? You probably haven't, yet you breathe about 17,000 times per day. But what if someone squeezed your throat and you couldn't breathe? It would most likely be the only thing you could think about. You may have seen the famous YouTube video by Eric Thomas, aka the Hip Hop Preacher, titled "When you want to succeed as bad as you want to breathe, then you will be successful."

The breath is the most essential thing in life. A human can go years without sunshine, weeks without food, days without water, but only minutes without air. This is a quintessential example of how we take the most magical and essential things in life for granted. I too took this natural technology for granted, but now I have a story to tell of how *conscious breathing* changed my life, as I believe it will change yours.

This book has very little to do with me, but more about you and your journey, since the breath is something we all intimately possess and share with one another. I will share some of my most profound stories with you, but not in an autobiographical way, more to show you how much I suffered, and what you have the ability to overcome with the natural healing technology that's flowing through your lungs as we interact.

> *"Show me a student with a powerful refined breathing practice, and I'll show you a person undergoing rapid transformation."*
> —Max Strom, *A Life Worth Breathing*

I'll be the first to admit, I'm a hard-headed, stubborn, quintessential Capricorn who's a very analytical and logical thinker. I was the type of person who needed to see it to believe it. Therefore, to believe that some silly breathing exercises could help heal my childhood trauma, melt away my anxiety, eradicate my panic attacks, give me million dollar business ideas and the motivation to carry them out, all while connecting me to a power that's greater than me, seemed a bit absurd to say the least, especially after I had experienced the powers of plant medicine and psychedelics. However, my journey and my discovery forced me to believe otherwise. Therefore I highly suggest that you stick around so I can share with you everything I learned within the contents of this book. All the knowledge and tools disclosed to you in these upcoming chapters have the power to transform your life if you put them into practice.

Don't worry, I hate boring books, so I'd never dare to write one; and, like you, I don't have time to read either. This is why I'm going to save you so much time and energy by giving you all the short-cuts, life-hacks, and everything you need to know about anxiety and healing with breathwork, all in one place, and in the most entertaining way possible. This book and my breathwork program are going to be nothing like you're expecting, but will be everything that you've been seeking. So buckle up and let's take this ride together. But before we begin this journey, I have something to say... ANXIETY SUCKS!

ANXIETY SUCKS!

Anxiety sucks! Plain and simple. It keeps us in our comfort zone and can truly ruin our quality of life, and we all have it to some degree. It's like spiritual sludge or black tar that drapes over us and prevents us from doing all the things we want to do that we know are good for us. I believe anxiety alone is the reason society drinks so much alcohol and does so many drugs. People just don't feel comfortable in their own bodies. Our system is so out of whack, and for so many different reasons (physically, chemically, and emotionally). Homeostasis is something we all seek; we just want to feel at home in our bodies: balanced, calm, clear-minded, and emotionally centered. Too many of us have this baseline "uneasy feeling," and we seek external stimuli to counterbalance this "off" feeling.

A drug and opioid epidemic is infiltrating the lives of many of our friends and family members. It affects more people than you think too; it's just that some are better at hiding it. In all earnestness, I believe no one is addicted to drugs. I believe they're addicted to escaping reality. They need to find ways to numb themselves or shift states of consciousness to escape their default feeling. Our natural state is supposed to be a neutral baseline of peace and equanimity, yet our default feeling is stressed, heavy, and lethargic. We struggle to muster the strength, energy, and motivation just to maintain our physical health and chase our passions, something that should be fun, enjoyable, and come naturally. So we have to ask ourselves, WHY is this? Why are we told to thrive in life yet everyone is struggling just to survive and get through the day? Well, let's look at the facts.

THE AGE OF ANXIETY

Five years ago, I read a study by The World Health Organization that said by the year 2020, anxiety and depression would be the #1 disabilities worldwide. Well, we've entered this new decade and these statistics have fully manifested. We're clearly living within this prophesied epidemic, solidified in such a way that our current era is being called *The Age of Anxiety.* Anxiety is born from stress. Stress can be easily managed and dealt with, but when unchecked, it accumulates and grows into a new monster called anxiety. When that anxiety goes unchecked, it grows into an even bigger, scarier monster known as depression.

My mother was a high school dropout and teenage runaway who got mixed up in the streets at a young age. Eventually, she decided to fix her life and go back to school, then she attended college to become a school teacher. When she first started teaching, she dealt with severe anxiety that turned into panic attacks and fainting spells. When she saw doctors, they prescribed antidepressants. She slowly became dependent on these meds, unbeknownst to her at the time.

Fast forward 17 years, when my mother evolved and became more conscious. It finally dawned on her that she was never depressed in the first place and only had anxiety, so why did they give her antidepressants? With this new self-awareness and introduction of the world wide web, she awakened and decided to get off the meds and live a more healthy and natural lifestyle. Little did she know that there were very few cases of people who've been on those meds for that long and were able to come off without becoming suicidal, and that's exactly what happened...

She tried to consult with various doctors and professionals but quickly learned that no one really knew more about antidepressant drugs and what they did long-term than she did. My mother soon discovered she was the only real professional because she had first-hand experience experimenting with just about every antidepressant medication in existence over the past 17 years. She knew more about the drugs and what they did than the doctors, both the good and the bad. Doctors could only extract the knowledge she had gained from her experiences for their own education. The irony is that my mother was never depressed to begin with but became severely depressed and suicidal only when she decided to get off the meds. It took her six years to wean off the pills. She had many close calls when she tried to take herself out, but she finally beat the monster.

I share this story with you in case you suffer from depression. No matter who thinks they understand what you're going through, they have no idea. They have no idea how dark and lonely that place can be. I share that story to let you know that I have tremendous compassion for people who suffer from depression, because I walked this path with my mother and tried to help her every step of the way. There was only so much I could do. There are no words to explain the empty and hopeless feeling a person with depression has. It's as if the world is in living color and they are seeing everything in black and white.

This is all relevant because studies show that people are more depressed today than they were during the Great Depression, and this was *before* the Coronavirus outbreak. It's so important to develop a practice to nip stress and anxiety in the bud now, before it evolves into something much worse down the road.

Unfortunately, the entire world is currently suffering from some form of S.A.D. (Stress, Anxiety, or Depression). In the next hour of you reading this, there will have been five suicides, and four out of the five will have been men. If you are male, or any gender thinking about committing suicide, hang in there, because I'm about to give you some life-changing tools to pull you out that quicksand so you can raise back up, stronger than ever.

According to an American Psychological Association survey, about one-fourth of Americans rate their stress level as 8 or more on a 10-point scale. In the U.S alone, over 40 million people suffer from some type of anxiety disorder. We're spending $42 billion a year in treatment, and over 9 million people are taking sleep aids. Yet the world is still miserable and needs a cup of coffee to get through the day. We have to ask ourselves, what the heck is really going on?

The answer is repressed trauma, unresolved pain, and much-needed emotional healing, all of which are leading to the physical and spiritual suffocation of our world.

NO ONE IS BREATHING ANYMORE!

Although humans can't survive without breathing, you'd be surprised how many are breathing just enough to keep themselves alive. Studies and statistics show we are using less and less of our lung capacity over time. The more stressed the world becomes, the less we breathe. This sounds ludicrous to say, but it's true; I too was one of these people.

I remember sitting at dinner with friends; it was actually my birthday. A friend was talking, and while she was talking, I noticed I was holding my breath the entire time. I looked down at my hand and saw that my left fist was clenched in a tight ball. I remember looking at my fist, shocked, as if it wasn't mine and I was looking at someone else's fist. I immediately released the death grip that was holding onto nothing but thin air. When I did, I suddenly gasped and took a deep breath, as if I had just surfaced from a deep sea dive. Nobody noticed this but me. Shortly following this self-realization, awareness began to emerge: "Was I just not breathing? How long was I holding my breath? Why the heck was I holding my breath? I wonder how long I've been doing this?"

"I've got to keep breathing. It'll be my worst business mistake if I don't."

—Steve Martin

While pondering this all day and night, I suddenly had a flashback from about a year ago, around the same time as my birthday. I was getting a massage, and the massage therapist kept telling me to *relax* and unclench my fist. She must have asked me four or five times, but I unknowingly kept closing it again. Finally she asked me, "What's going on, hon? What are you holding onto?" I trivialized my response and brushed it off, but in hindsight, she was onto something. Why was I clenching my fist? What *was* I holding onto?

I noticed that past year (or more), I was grinding my teeth, clenching my fist, and holding my breath... all while trying to live a normal and productive life. The question became WHY? What would cause someone to do this?

I later found that these types of unconscious behaviors are linked to one another. The breath-holding is a form of self-suffocation and self-sabotage that inadvertently allows toxins to accumulate in the body that directly affect our mental state and nervous system. The fist-clenching was me literally holding onto something I wasn't ready to let go of (pain, sadness, guilt, shame, or whatever), the emotional chains of the past. The teeth grinding was connected to indecision, the inability to process repressed emotions, along with the inaction of clearing that trauma out of my system.

I learned that everything was connected. When we have some form of unresolved trauma trapped in our body, it tightens up our diaphragms, clogs our energy channels, restricts our breathing, and causes tension in the body. However, these are just the beginning stages. If gone unchecked, these physical warnings can fester into worse conditions. This can go unnoticed for years. Only self-diagnosis through self-awareness will save you (this is key). Meaning, you could be suffering from all of the aforementioned right now and not even know it, because you either don't have a good sense of body-awareness, or you've shut off the switch in the brain a long time ago to cope with the pain. The brain is very good at doing this, not because it wants to harm you; it's the opposite. The brain protects you by any means necessary, even if it requires shutting off sensors in the body or burying unprocessed emotions deep in our tissues and unconscious mind to prevent pain and suffering. Since the breath is the physical manifestation of the energetic flow in our body, poor breathing habits are usually the first indication that something needs to be cleared from our energy field.

The entire world is in denial about forgetting how to breathe, and I don't blame them. If you were to tell someone, "Hey man, you're breathing all wrong," they'd look at you like you're the crazy one. The bottom line is you can't come up with a solution if you don't recognize the problem, because you can't fix something if you don't know it is broken. This is why the breath is the last thing people look at, when it should be the first. The answer is hiding in plain sight and "right under your nose."

At all my breathwork events, I have everyone take a deep breath on three. When they do, I can see everyone's chest expand and stomachs suck in. This is a sign of respiratory distress called *paradoxical breathing,* and more people have it than those who don't.

When taking a breath, the abdominal wall and the chest wall should expand and move out, not in. If you were to watch a fish, a dog, or a baby breathe, you would see when they inhale their belly rises (not sinks). As we get older, we experience trauma and begin to collect and store these emotions in the body, which causes this dysfunctional breathing. It also doesn't help that men subconsciously tend to puff up their chest, and women tend to suck in their bellies.

Energy flows up from the pelvis and must travel through the diaphragm in order to get through to the heart. Our first defense area is our power center (stomach). If we sense danger to the emotional expression of this feeling, we will contract our diaphragm and shorten our breath to prevent feeling this emotion. This traps the energy in our Personal Power area and causes acute respiratory issues. We *think* we're breathing just fine, when in fact the body is in distress and calling for help. We're no longer expanding our diaphragms and breathing into the most powerful place in our entire body, the belly!

TRUST YOUR GUT

The main reason you should breathe into your belly is because most likely you're not breathing into it anymore. When we breathe low and slow into the belly, it's called *Diaphragmatic Breathing*, aka belly breathing. Your stomach is your power center! When a professional fighter wins a championship they don't give them a trophy for their mantel, they give them a belt that wraps around their waist. This belt symbolizes power. Your stomach is home to all your *chi*, *prana*, and vital life force energy.

Over 80% of your serotonin is produced in your gut, and over 80% of your immune system is in your gut. These two elements are the most significant elements that produce the two things we seek most: health and happiness.

Diaphragmatic breathing is the best type of breathing to relieve stress and anxiety, and this is the type of breathing we focus on in the breathwork detox program. Diaphragmatic belly breathing is also very effective for grounding. Grounding is very important in becoming centered and balanced in the present. This is significant for anxiety since anxiety stems from constantly worrying about the future.

Humans are a bio battery where energy can be charged and stored. According to the famous Taoist Master, Mantak Chia, the gut is the only place in the body where this energy is stored. The chi (prana) in the stomach has positive and negative charges that can cultivate chi. Chi is our lifeforce; it's our bioelectric magnetic power. The Chinese call it chi, Indians call it prana, and Amercans call it energy, or electromagnetic power.

The University of California, Berkeley has found that hundreds of different bacteria in the human gut are electrogenic (they produce a change in the electrical potential of a cell). *Medical News Today* on September 13, 2018 posted an article stating that "a new study has made a surprising discovery: numerous gut bacteria of many kinds are able to generate electricity." The article stated they're now looking for ways to develop alternative, more sustainable battery-like devices with this finding. This paper can also be found in the journal *Nature.*

In the practice of Tai chi, acupuncture, and Chinese medicine, the area behind the belly button is called the "windpipe." This is the area where all the body's chi flows in and out. If you press down on this area in your tummy and it hurts, it's a good indication that you have *stagnant chi*. This means your windpipe is blocked and old chi cannot leave, which means new chi cannot enter. If this is the case, your entire digestive system, peristalsis, nutrient absorption, and elimination slows, which affects your energy levels and mental clarity.

Your stomach and digestion are crucial to your health and well-being. When detoxing, naturopathic doctors will always say you should do a colon cleanse before any type of detox such as liver, kidney, blood, etc. If you want to cleanse the mind, you must cleanse the gut first. The brain and the gut are interconnected; when a patient suffers a traumatic brain injury, within two hours they also have leaky gut syndrome.

The stomach is known as the second brain. There is an intelligence in the gut, which is why you've probably heard the phrase, "trust your gut." You've never heard someone say "trust your elbow" or "trust your liver." There's a technology in the gut that is pivotal to your energetic makeup and intuition. When you listen to your gut feeling, you are tapping into the intelligence of your body and your emotions.

> *"In religion we call it spirits. In science we call it energy. In the streets we call it vibes. Whatever you call it, all I'm saying is trust it."*
>
> —Unknown

Science has not fully discovered the intelligence of the gut. In 2016, they discovered a new organ in the gut never acknowledged before. It's called the *mesentery*, which controls all digestion, absorption, and elimination. You're probably thinking exactly what I was thinking when I heard this: "How the heck did it take them so long to discover an entire organ? Where was it hiding? And how can an organ with such significance be overlooked for so many years?"

There is so much that western science chooses not to acknowledge due to traditional teachings and outdated core beliefs. One of the most astounding and unacknowledged findings is the knowledge of *kundalini*, *nadis*, and *chakras*, which breathwork directly affects. Our sacral chakra, also known as our sexual chakra, is located in the belly around the navel. When we have stomach issues or prana/chi blockages in that area, chances are we have some sort of sexual dysfunction as well because the two are synonymous. The goal is to get our sexual energy (kundalini energy) and our heart energy in sync and flowing to one another so deep healing can occur.

People don't understand how interconnected, intelligent, and significant the stomach is for health and vitality. We've lost touch with our power and forgotten how to breathe. By doing so, we're faced with the challenge of ignorance, because you can't fix something if you don't think there's anything wrong with it. I can say this with confidence. I was this person who didn't think anything was wrong with me. I was young, healthy, and in shape, but unbeknownst to me, my engine light was on, my transmission was slipping, and my gas tank was running on fumes. Little did I know it was only a matter of time before my system would crash and break down.

PUNCHED IN THE GUT

"Everyone has a plan until they get punched in the face."

—Mike Tyson

When I visited India, just a few days after returning I was sitting at my computer. Out of nowhere, I felt like I got punched in the stomach. This feeling stopped me in my tracks. After about a week of discomfort, I finally went to the doctor and had an ultrasound done. They couldn't find anything wrong with me. However, not long after, when I began to eat food, I would get deathly sick and extremely lethargic afterward. This forced me to change my diet to lighter foods. Slowly I went from carnivore, to pescatarian, to vegetarian, then to vegan for eight months, before becoming a flexitarian (conscious eater).

The stomach pain I had experienced soon transformed into a strange tingling sensation in my belly that would make my entire body vibrate and my tongue taste like there was metal in my mouth. Doctors thought I was crazy, but it felt as if there were hundreds of spiders crawling inside my stomach. I was convinced I had heavy metal poisoning or contracted parasites from traveling to India. However, the doctors couldn't find any traces of heavy metals or parasites, so they ordered various other tests to properly diagnose me. This included stool, blood, urine, and hair tests. They found nothing! The conditions were getting worse and I started to lose large amounts of weight. I began electing for discovery surgeries, such as a colonoscopy, endoscopy, and I even swallowed two giant pills that were cameras that could look inside my small intestine. Again, they found nothing and started sending me to specialists such as neurologists and gastrointestinal (G.I.) experts. All my tests came up negative, so I began demanding double-testing and second opinions and still came up empty-handed. One day a doctor told me, "Kurtis, I'm sorry, but there's nothing we can do for you anymore. To be honest with you, you're healthier than I am."

That is the worst thing a doctor can tell you when you are suffering and in pain. They believed I was psychosomatic. As crazy as it sounds, deep down I was actually waiting and wanting a doctor to tell me that I had some crazy disease. To me, it would have been better than everyone thinking it was all in my head while I suffered internally. The pain was mysterious and enigmatic. Realistically speaking, on the physical pain scale from 1-10, mine was probably a 6, but the strange feeling that it was giving me and the thoughts it was provoking made it a solid 10. It was such a foreign feeling, and something I had never felt before. If I could describe it in just one word, I would call it TORTUROUS!

This caused me to embark on a personal healing journey around the world, which led me to some of the most profound alternative modalities on the planet. I took classes, courses, and was trained by everyone from holistic doctors to shamans. I began collecting certifications: NLP, Life Coaching, Hypnotherapy, Reiki I, Reiki II, Reiki Master, Avatar Masters Course, International Sports Science & Fitness, you name it! But nothing seemed to work for me. I drank ayahuasca 14 times, smoked DMT, Changa, and Bufo. I fasted for 21 days and did the most robust parasite cleanses on earth. I even had shamans burn me with tiny sticks and put frog

venom on the open wound, which causes you to start vom-
iting the bile and toxins from the body (gross—I know). The
point is, I was dedicated, dedicated to discovering the most
profound healing modalities on the planet to seek relief. I felt
I did everything I could, even if it was bizarre and invasive,
because when you are desperate you will try anything.

I was so desperate that one day I just said, "Enough!" I
checked myself into the E.R. and asked the doctors for an
emergency surgery where they would cut open my stomach just to see what was inside. I was convinced it was
some highly-intelligent stealth-parasite that knew how to
evade human medical technology, possibly a new species
never discovered before by mankind. However, the doctors
wouldn't do the surgery, and I'm glad they didn't.

THE GAME CHANGER

That week I sought temporary relief and started going to an amazing "tummy massager" named Jannica in Los Angeles. Her modality was called *Chi Nei Tsang* (CNT). It's a highly effective centuries-old Toaist abdominal release and healing touch therapy from China. She told me the area behind my belly button, which she called my "windpipe," was very tight and my chi was blocked.

In conjunction with my tummy massages, she recommended I try something called breathwork. I immediately dismissed it because, let's face it, the word breathwork just doesn't sound too appealing. Plus, what could breathing do for me that pills, surgery, Kambo, DMT, ayahuasca, or Bufo couldn't do? But I took her advice and went to a workshop. I was still desperate and was willing to try anything with just a hope of relief.

When I arrived at the workshop, sitting next to me was a tiny 90-pound female to my left, and a giant NFL football player to my right. About 15 minutes into the breathwork, the girl to my left started bawling her eyes out. I remember saying to myself, "Man, this girl must have had a bad day." Then just five minutes into her crying, the big guy to my right started weeping like a baby too. I wondered what was going on. As the thought came into my mind, "What the heck is going on here? Why is everyone cryyyyyyy..." and before I could finish that thought, I belted out and started crying right along with them. I had the most profound life-changing experience lying on the yoga mat that night, "just breathing." At that moment, I knew I had to share this modality with the world.

MY AHA MOMENT!

When the event ended and I went home, I noticed my stomach pain was gone. When I woke up, it was still gone. I couldn't believe it. I was more shocked than relieved at that moment. As the day went on, I began to sense a strange feeling in my back. The feeling was so strange, yet so familiar. It felt like I had an orgasm stuck inside my back that I couldn't get out, but my stomach was fine. It was as if that strange pain and all my anxiety migrated from my stomach to the area between my shoulder blades. The more breathwork I did on my own, the more this energy would move around in my body. Then it finally hit me! The reason doctors couldn't find anything wrong with me was because my issue wasn't physical; it was emotional! My condition was an energetic disease due to trapped emotions and trauma in my body. This was causing stagnant energy and chi to build up and block my energetic pathways.

I later found out this energy was called kundalini. As I did more breathwork, my kundalini activated and the energy started to release. I cried, I shook, I awakened, and I finally began to heal. The breath became my teacher and my healer.

LET'S NOT CALL IT GOD[1]

"Student, tell me, what is God? He is the breath inside the breath."

—Kabir

The single most sacred and intimate thing humans share is breath. It's the spiritual web that connects all things. It's the one thing that connects us all and that we need the most.

In my book *The World is Yours, The Secrets Behind "The Secret,"* I wrote about a colony of Quaking Aspens, now called Pando, located in Fishlake National Forest in Utah. Researchers and scientists couldn't figure out why each of the trees in the colony looked similar and had identical genetic markers throughout the entire forest, miles apart

---

1 Will Henshall, in conversation with the author.

from one another. They eventually discovered that the trees shared a single massive underground root system, with all the trees connected as one giant tree. The root system of Pando is estimated to be eighty thousand years old, but it took until 1992 to declare it the oldest and largest living organism in the world. Just as we recently made the great Pando tree discovery, I believe humanity will soon discover we are all one, we are all connected to one another, and we always have been.

The trees inhale the same breath that you exhale. Other animals inhale the same breath you exhale. The breath that is in you now was in someone else earlier. You share the same air as your best friend and your worst enemy. You share the same breath that Jesus, Hitler, Moses, Buddha, and Gandhi all breathed. This is the circle of life. Without this natural eb and flow, all things would cease to exist.

> *"The Tao is the breath that never dies. It is the mother of all creation. It is the root and ground of every soul. The fountain of Heaven and Earth laid open."*
> —Tao Te Ching Verse 6

Breathing is the language of the soul. No matter our religious beliefs, we must realize that ultimately we all come from the same place. We all have a spark of life force from the creator within us. This life force is called our chi, prana, and is the elemental force that distributes energy throughout our body.

Many ancient languages associate breath and spirit, or breath and soul, as the same word. Spiritus comes from an old Latin word, meaning "to breathe" but also [meaning] "soul" or "spirit." Another example is aloha which originally meant, "breath of God" in ancient Hawaiian. So, when we say aloha to each other, it essentially means "I breathe God with you." It seems … that human beings understand the act of breathing to be much more than mere physical survival, but as an intimate connection with the divine source, and that breath is actually associated with spiritual life.

—Max Strom[2]

Take the example of our Prime Creator (Source, God, or whatever you choose to call this energy) as all-powerful and ubiquitous (everywhere), yet invisible. Imagine this God-like energy being essential for all beings to survive. Imagine this energy extending from our earth plane into the infinite cosmos, yet residing inside all of mankind. Could you not say the same thing about the breath? Could this be why the Bible says "The kingdom of God is within you" and why God's "kingdom shall have no end?"

The very first thing you did when you came into this world was inhale your first breath; the very last thing you will do when you leave will be to exhale one last breath. Is this why they say God is with you from the very beginning until the very end?

"And the Lord God formed man of the dust of the ground, and breathed into his nostrils the breath of life; and man became a living soul."

—Genesis 2:7 ASV

2 Strom, Max. *A Life Worth Breathing: A Yoga Master's Handbook of Strength, Grace, and Healing.* New York, NY. Skyhorse Publishing, 2012.

A life force energy and healing power is encoded into our breath. Whenever we need to be centered, we can always turn to the breath. The breath teaches us to be present. We cannot retrieve a breath from yesterday nor save a breath for tomorrow. We can only focus on the breath that is happening now.

THE POWER OF THE BREATH

Navy Seals train in various breathing exercises to help them to energize themselves, calm their nerves, and gain extreme laser focus. Navy Seals use only the best of the best, fastest, and most efficient technologies in the world. The breath is that technology! Breath control (*pranayama*) is their go-to modality in dire times. If you ever watched *American Sniper,* you know a sniper's superpower is their breath. They shoot in the stillness, the neutral space between each breath and each heartbeat.

> *"We master our breath, we master our mind."*
> —*American Sniper*

We all have fingerprints, footprints, and breathprints. There is a unique pattern to how we breathe and how our breath reacts in certain situations. The difference between a fingerprint and a breathprint is that your breathprint can change. Breathing is one of the only systems in our body that is automatic yet voluntary; we have control over it. In other words, we can consciously control our breath and create new habits through breath-training.

Ten percent of life is what happens to us, and the remaining ninety percent is how we react to it. Every trigger has the potential to make you bigger. Between the trigger and your response is a small window, a space of opportunity. In that small space lies your power, your free will to choose how you respond. In your response lies your destiny, freedom, and free will to evolve or repeat karmic cycles.

Our breath is usually the first responder at every "crime scene." When the breath responds, it tells the body how to respond. The breath is a great mediator that can calm the situation or freak everyone out and instigate a fight or flight response.

I attended a breathwork masterclass with Dan Brulé and he explained that through the breath (pranayama), we can train ourselves to react differently in the same situation, similar to police training. If you or I heard a gun in the mall, we would most likely run as far away from that sound as possible, while police officers hear gunshots and run towards the sound. Similarly, we can retrain our breath. We must reprogram the breath so it's working for us and not against us. The breath is always working, but the question is, are *we* breathing the breath or is the *breath* breathing us? After all, the breath is ALWAYS with you, in every situation, so training the breath is something worth learning.

"If you're going to master anything, master the breath."
—Tony Robbins, in *Just Breathe* by Dan Brulé

Pranayama (breathwork) is so easy, yet so effective. It's our original medicine. You'd be amazed at what monks can do with the breath. Monks on YouTube can channel chi from their hand and set a piece of paper on fire with it. Other monks can dry a soaking wet bed sheet in 0 degrees celsius in just minutes. This is all possible by mastering the breath.

Here are some areas of life and professions where the breath is a focal point for mastery:

- Anger Management
- Attention Training
- Childbirth
- Corporate Mindfulness Training
- Fitness Trainers
- Hypnotherapists
- Holistic Healers
- Meditation
- Military Training
- Martial Artists
- Olympic Athletes
- Peak Performers
- Personal Development
- Public Speaking
- Professional Athletes
- Situational Coaching
- Spiritual Development
- Yoga Practitioners

BREATHWORK MISCONCEPTIONS

Since breathwork is very powerful and many have profound cathartic experiences, someone always asks the question, "How safe is this?" Rest assured: there have been zero reported cases of heart attacks, strokes, or other serious side effects caused from breathing. Therefore, it seems it is quite safe for most healthy people.

Breathwork does not cause hyperventilation because you inhale right after you exhale, without waiting for the carbon dioxide levels to rise, which avoids some of the negative effects of hyperventilation. Hyperventilating is when you exhale more oxygen than you inhale. The intention and goal of breathwork is the opposite: to take IN as much oxygen as possible. Basically, you can't die from breathing, but you can definitely die from not breathing.

Breathing is the closest thing to doing nothing when you're doing something, but I can almost guarantee you that breathwork is going to be NOTHING like you're expecting. After all, the most common reaction people have who have taken one of my workshops is, "WOW, that wasn't what I was expecting!" Breathwork is profound yet extremely simple, but don't get that confused with being easy.

The greatest misconception about breathwork is that people think they've already tried it, until they actually try it. It's very cathartic and doesn't compare to any other form of breathing or pranayama such as "Yoga Breathing," "Kundalini Breathing," "Alternate Nostril Breathing," "Breath of Fire," or any other form of breathing practice, which we'll discuss later. Breathwork is a uniquely powerful and profound experience.

IS BREATHWORK FOR ME?

Are you breathing? Do you want to create radical transformation in your life? Are you willing to try something new? If you answered YES to any of those questions, you should do everything in your power and see why breathwork is beginning to explode around the globe.

BREATHWORK, THE NEW YOGA!

A massive revolution is on the rise! The popularity of breathwork is exploding. You've either just started hearing about Breathwork Detox, or you've had the pleasure of discovering it on your own. If not, the only true way of knowing the power of Breathwork Detox is to experience it for yourself.

Humanity is currently living in its highest states of consciousness. More than ever, you'll hear people talk about "energy." If you want to truly experience what pure life-force energy feels like surging through your body, try breathwork! Whether you believe in this energy or not, you will be changed by breathwork in some fashion, and you will notice this change almost immediately. I believe breathwork has the power to change the world, and I say this without vacillation.

"...your breath melts the ego, almost like fire melts ice."
—Max Strom, *A Life Worth Breathing*

Trying to explain the feeling you have after a breathwork session is like trying to explain a kaleidoscope to a blind person…it's virtually impossible! Nevertheless, let me try to explain the unexplainable.

SO WHAT IS BREATHWORK EXACTLY?

The question should really be, what *isn't* breathwork? Breathwork is beneficial in so many ways. It's easy to do, yet so powerful and profound, and still hardly anybody knows about it.

"Breathwork is like 20 years of therapy in one night without saying a word."
—A Breathwork Student

The term *breathwork* is a rebranded term, but the practice originates from India and has been around for thousands of years. It's a modernized form of pranayama, the control and regulation of the breath through certain techniques and exercises. *Prana* means breath or vital energy, and *ayama* means control. So pranayama is the ability to control the movement of the lifeforce energy in your body using intention and focus in unison with the breath. Breathwork is a very specific version of pranayama, which I believe is one of the most transformative.

Breathwork is **expanding for the mind** because it brings profound mental clarity and creativity. It connects you to a deeper, more evolved part of yourself, a power greater than you.

Breathwork releases certain chemicals into the brain that enhance our mood, leaving us with **euphoric feelings of bliss** that linger for days or weeks after. They say some doors only open from the inside; BREATHWORK is the key to accessing that doorway. It is a highly effective and powerful tool for accessing the subconscious mind and clearing out any unhealthy belief systems that have been getting in our way.

> *"It's the one physical thing in our bodies that we can access easily which links the conscious and unconscious processes of the brain."*
> —Dr. Alan Hobson, M.D., a leading brain researcher
> at Harvard, quoted by Dr. Dani Gordon, M.D.

Breathwork is very cathartic and provides **deep healing for the body.** It helps release any stored memories, emotions, trauma, or stagnant energies that may be trapped almost *instantaneously.* These energetic blockages hinder our spiritual growth, drain our energy, and affect our physical and mental well-being, which can eventually evolve from fatigue into dis-ease or illness.

By oxygenating the entire body using a very specific breathwork technique, you are able to tap into the unconscious parts of yourself where these blockages reside and clear them out.

Breathwork revitalizes your spirit with euphoric feelings of love, gratitude, and bliss. The best part about breathwork is that all of the aforementioned can occur in just ONE session. You don't have to be practicing for years; all you have to do is go in with an open mind and you may just have one of the most profound life-changing experiences you've ever had. The practice of breathwork has birthed thousands of testimonials from people all over the world with life-altering stories. Here are just a few:

"Absolutely speechless! I can't express the amount of gratitude, love, and kindness I have for what Kurtis Thomas has created. Breathwork through Kurtis has changed my life and I recommend everyone who wants to take their life to the next level to attend his events!"

—Bret Lockett, Financial Advisor & Former New England Patriot Football Player

"The feelings I felt during (and after) the session could best be described as one of the most divine, life-altering experiences of truth and oneness; something I've only experienced a handful of times prior to my breathwork session with Kurtis."

—Dragan Trajkovski, Team Tony Robbins

"I've taken various breathwork classes and I've tried many detoxes...Kurtis' Breathwork Detox was by far was the most powerful I've ever experienced. I wish I had known about this sooner, but I'm so glad this is a part of my now and my forever."

—Kimberly Glass, 2008 Beijing Olympics, Silver Medalist in Volleyball

"I can't remember the last time I felt this good. The experience almost feels surreal and words don't really do it justice. Kurtis is a master of his craft and I can't recommend Breathwork enough."
—Rob Harrand, Major League Baseball Pitcher

Breathwork is not woo-woo hippie stuff. Research proves its benefits: helping alleviate accumulated stress, reducing or eliminating chronic anxiety, and calming panic attacks. I am a beneficiary of this phenomenon. The Breathwork Detox achieves such great results because it induces a catharsis and energetic release that helps eradicate emotional trauma and clear the energetic pathways in the body.

"[Breathwork] is also one of my favourite ways to hit the 'reset' button, and re-energize after a stressful day or week and release tension that you don't even realize you are holding onto until it's gone!"
—Dr. Dani Gordon, MD

"There are many rivers that lead to the ocean and Kurtis' breathwork is a waterfall of energy shifting transformation."
—Dr. Varshini

The great thing about breathwork is that anyone can do it, anytime, anywhere, and it's always highly effective. It's an untapped superpower that's extremely easy with some of the most profound results. Many people say that breathwork is much easier for them than yoga or meditation. In the next chapter, we'll discuss how breathwork compares to meditation...

BREATHWORK VS. MEDITATION

"You should sit in meditation for twenty minutes everyday—unless you're too busy; then you should sit for an hour."

—Dr. Sukhraj Dhillon

I live in Los Angeles where everyone works out and is in shape. When L.A. people work out, they want to see a muscle, and they want to see it fast. It's the same with the results of meditation. Breathwork is like meditation on steroids! Breathwork is for people who don't like to meditate but want to see instant results, not results two years from now. The great thing about the Breathwork Detox is that the results are immediate and undeniable.

I believe meditation is more of an advanced practice. I say that because we live in "the age of anxiety," and if you try to get someone who's chronically stressed to "sit down, sit still, and don't think a thought for the next 20 minutes," they are going to get even more stressed out! Our minds are already overactive with so many wild and crazy untamed thoughts.

It's safe to say we all may need a little "brain-washing" at first. That is why I no longer recommend meditation to beginners. I prefer to give them the tool of breathwork first. When they've cleaned out their system via Breathwork Detox, they can implement meditation afterward, and it will be much easier, more effective, and probably more enjoyable.

Both breathwork and meditation are great tools that serve their purpose, but they need to be implemented appropriately. Trying to meditate without doing a deep clean is like trying to wax a dirty car. Breathwork is like cleaning your car with a power washer, while meditation is like trying to clean your car with a toothbrush. Think of breathwork like deep cleaning, while meditation is the maintenance.

I've also noticed that people who suffer from ADD and ADHD love breathwork because it's much easier to do with distractions and a scattered mind than meditation. Mediation is sometimes unpredictable; there's a barrier to entry that breathwork doesn't have.

Meditation is usually done sitting in silence in an upright position, while breathwork is done lying on your back on a yoga mat in a comfortable position. Meditation is done in silence, while breathwork suggests music. The music is played for motivational purposes to help release trapped emotions by tapping into the energy and emotion of those particular songs.

BREATHWORK 101

here are many names for breathwork and it can get a bit confusing. You may have heard these terms before: "Rebirthing Breathwork," "Transformational Breathwork," "Shamanic Breathwork," or "Clarity Breathwork." Breathwork is simply the umbrella term used for these various types of breathing practices. Some are more well-known than others and are practiced more widely. Although each method has its own characteristics and unique elements, they all share various healing aspects with many therapeutic overlaps.

HERE IS A LIST OF POPULAR
BREATHWORK MODALITIES (A-Z):

Breatharian isn't a breathwork modality but more of a very rare lifestyle that I've included just to show the power of the breath. The term *Breatharian* is very controversial. It's a lifestyle through which a person can reach levels of consciousness where they can obtain all survival sustenance from simply the breath (prana) and sunlight alone. This means they can live on just herbs, some without consuming food, and in some cases, very little to no water. I know all of this seems like major woo-woo; however, I've met one breatharian in Sedona, Arizona and there are many in India. American theoretician and physicist, Nassim Haramein, founder of the Resonance Science Foundation, is a former breatharian who speaks on this practice in some of his keynote speeches.

Breathwork Detox is a powerful full-body cleanse using the prana energy of the breath. It's a multi-faceted physical, mental, emotional, and spiritual all-in-one detox. I guide my students through this entire process using powerful motivational messages and NLP techniques to help break up old neuropathways of the brain. Breathwork Detox uses specific detoxifying essential oils in conjunction with the breath to open up the energetic pathways and reinforce healing.

The beauty of Breathwork Detox is that I've studied all of the other modalities for you so that you don't have to. I took the most effective aspects of multiple practices throughout generations and consolidated them into ONE powerful, yet simple breathwork protocol, with a modern twist of my own style and flavor. The goal was to not only make it more unique, but to be the most effective in the shortest amount of time.

Clarity Breathwork evolved out of "Rebirthing Breathwork" and essentially has the same benefits. The founders of Clarity Breathwork found the term "Rebirthing" limiting in its implications for healing birth trauma and wanted to encompass a much wider range of issues.

The name they chose, "Clarity Breathwork," was chosen to emphasize the change in consciousness that results from the breathwork process and to stay away from Rebirthing's emphasis on physical immortality.

DMT Breathing—(see Breathwork is Trippy on page 73)

Holotropic Breathwork is a name that seems to pop up frequently on Google searches, or when people are discussing breathwork. The name *Holotropic* literally means "moving toward wholeness" (from the Greek "*holos*"= whole, and "*trepein*"= moving in the direction of something). What differentiates Holotropic Breathing from Breathwork Detox is the pace and the time allotted. Holotropic breathing is done at a much faster pace and is done for a longer period of time, usually in an all-day workshop that includes the construction and sharing of Mandala artwork afterward. This makes for a great workshop; however, many people don't have this amount of time and prefer an hour-long class that yields the same results.

Integrative Breathwork is derived from the Holotropic method and philosophy. This method isn't as popular as the others but still notable enough to make it on the list.

Rebirthing Breathwork is one of the most notable and long-standing breathwork practices that's done through both the nose and the mouth. The word "rebirthing" can sometimes intimidate new breathers because it sounds pretty intense. When many people, especially women, think about "birthing," conflicting pleasurable and painful memories arise (which we all know will result in a beautiful outcome). Rebirthing is done two ways: wet rebirthing and dry rebirthing. Wet rebirthing is done in a hot tub or a pool, sometimes requiring the participant to be completely nude, and sometimes the facilitator as well. This type of rebirthing isn't for everybody and isn't necessary to have a transformational experience. However, the founder of rebirthing did a great job of getting breathwork out to the world, and he is definitely a staple in this practice. It's worthy to note that many breathwork modalities derived from this practice.

Shamanic Breathwork is a process to awaken the healer and shaman within. This breathwork modality consists of tribal music and shamanic drumming. Although I've worked closely with shamans for almost a decade and highly respect this lifestyle, many people don't want to be considered a Shaman but still want the benefits of Shamanic Breathwork. Shamanic Breathwork is highly effective, but the name can be intimidating. If you're looking for a tribal and grounding breathwork practice, this may be one worth trying. One of my goals with the Breathwork Detox was to deliver these same powerful benefits in a much more modernized approach for the masses.

Transformational Breathwork is transformational indeed! Although this method of breathwork has many parts and levels, it can get confusing for new breathers. Transformational Breathwork incorporates tapping, toning (humming certain sounds for a long period of time), and conscious invocation.

Wim Hof Method is considered a breathwork modality now. Many people ask me how Breathwork Detox compares to this method. First, I will say that I'm a fan of the Ice Man's work, and there are parts of his modality that I love and others I choose to leave out. His breathing method incorporates breath holds and sets instead of circular connected breathing. Breath holds are great; however, when the conscious mind is focusing on counting numbers and trying to figure out what set it is on, overthinking and confusion often removes the transcendental part of breathwork that I like to call "the downloads." Downloads are instant connections to profound information within the subconscious mind that provide epiphanies, realizations, and clarity connected to one's mission and purpose. One of the main reasons I do breathwork every morning is for these daily downloads (they're priceless to me). What I love about Wim is his approach and the advice he gives to people who aren't sure if they're breathing right: "It doesn't matter. Just breathe mother f*ckers!" Priceless!

Buteyko Breathing Method is a very unique style of breathwork that involves breath control and breath-holding exercises. Studies show it has been used successfully as a therapy to treat people with asthma. I must say I'm quite biased against this method of breathing, considering many of my health conditions came from NOT breathing. However, its popularity has grown, and I believe it deserves a worthy mention. If you're not an Olympic swimmer or professional scuba diver, and the Buteyko Method doesn't excite you, you may want to look into practicing "stomach vacuums" instead. Stomach vacuums involve short breath holds but with many other digestive benefits that can complement your breathwork practice.

Yoga Breathing is probably the most popular out of all the aforementioned modalities. However, "Yoga Breathing" is very vague and is also an umbrella term similar to "breathwork" like "fitness" is. Unlike meditation and yoga, which can take months or even years to have profound breakthroughs, breathwork is a multifaceted process specifically designed to effectively remove mental and emotional blockages in a very efficient way.

Breathwork is a powerful and profound experience that shouldn't be compared to "Yoga Breathing," "Kundalini Breathing," "Alternate Nostril Breathing," "Breath of Fire," "Zen Yoga Breathing," or any other form of yoga breathing practices. Although I use these other forms of breathing for different occasions, Yoga Breathing and breathwork are like apples and oranges: similar but very different.

"Breath of Fire" is the closest method to breathwork, yet it's very different. Breath of Fire is power breathing with a focus on pushing out the exhale, while breathwork is the complete opposite. The goal of breathwork is focusing on the inhale and oxygenating the entire body as much as possible for the most radical healing benefits.

BEGINNING A BREATHWORK PRACTICE:

How often should you practice breathwork? The answer is as much as you can! Developing a breathwork practice is like building a relationship; the more time you spend with someone the stronger your bond becomes and the deeper the connection grows.

Making breathwork a daily habit will reap the most benefits. A full breathwork detox session is about 27-30 minutes of active detox breathing; a shortened session is about 7-10 minutes. Best case scenario would be a commitment to a full breathwork session everyday. 1-3 full sessions per week is sufficient for a powerful practice if it's mixed with shortened 7-10 minute sessions on your off-days.

PREPARING FOR A BREATHWORK SESSION:

Find a comfortable place in your home where you won't have any distractions. This area will be the sacred space where your breathwork practice lives and grows.

TIP: It's advantageous to dedicate an exact time every day to practice breathwork and to stay consistent with that allocated time slot.

- You will need a YOGA MAT or somewhere comfortable to lie down on your back, such as a bed or a couch (no pillows are needed for your neck).

- You may want to put a pillow or bolster under your knees if you have lower back pain.

- Dress comfortably and wear multiple layers that can be removed easily. (Women should not wear any eye makeup. Crying during breathwork is common.)

- A BLANKET is always nice (or wear many warm layers that can be taken off). The body's temperature tends to drop during breathwork, and when it does, you'll be happy you took this advice.

- SLEEP EYE MASK: If you have an eye mask or sleep mask, consider wearing it to help you go deeper. They're under $10 and you can get them on Amazon.com. Try breathwork with and without an eye mask to see which method you prefer.

- A MUSIC PLAYER (your cellphone is fine).

- Bluetooth speaker or headphones to play your guided breathwork session.

- Drink lots of water the night before and right after breathwork.

- Epson salt baths are great after an intense breathwork session.

- Make sure you have everything you need the night before (yoga mat, blanket, eye-mask, music player, bluetooth or headphones, essential oils, notepad, pen, etc.) This removes any barriers to entry that may subconsciously prevent you from establishing a dedicated practice.

- DON'T EAT RIGHT BEFORE BREATHWORK. Breathwork is best on an empty stomach. You want your last meal to be 2-3 hours prior to Breathwork (the emptier your stomach, the better your results). If you must eat something to stabilize your blood sugar, then make it something light.

HOW TO BREATHE DURING BREATHWORK

- Relax your jaw and open your mouth a bit wider than what feels normal.

- Don't tense the muscles in your face while breathing, because it makes the body think it's in danger.

- Breathe in through your mouth, deep into your belly, then top it off by filling your chest with air until you're completely filled with oxygen, then let the exhale fall out (don't push the exhale out).

- The breath must stay connected. There is no pause or hesitation between breaths. It's a constant loop of circular breathing.

- Take two (2) deep breaths in instead of one fast one, because gasping for air is an emergency signal to the brain.

- Remember, you are in control and the speed is up to you; you can slow down or speed up the ride as you wish. Fast and full will help you go deeper into your healing and can lead to more breakthroughs. Breathing low and slow but fully for a longer period of time is better for relaxation and pleasure.

- At any time you can slow or stop the process by breathing in and out through your nose instead of your mouth.

Please note that there are some powerful effects that happen during a breathwork practice that I thoroughly explain in the beginning of my classes and workshops. I usually spend 20-30 minutes setting the context for your breathwork session while explaining all the things that can happen during breathwork and what to expect if you wish to have a breakthrough. This introduction is crucial to the success of a person's breathwork, especially if they're new to breathwork and have no idea what to expect.

Your first breathwork journey should be experienced in a yoga studio or in a virtual breathwork class by a trained professional who can coach you before, during, and after your breathwork session. I highly recommend not practicing breathwork for the first time without an instructor or someone who can hold space for you and guide you each step of the way.

To watch a video of me showing you "How to Do Breathwork" along with suggestions on "Before Breathwork TIPS" and "After Breathwork TIPS," plus a Bonus video on "Grounding exercises," you can join me in my next online Breathwork Detox class here https://linktr.ee/manfromthestars, or enroll in my Breathwork Detox program at www.BreathworkDetox. com, where I give you all the tools, guidance, and support you'll need to start a powerful breathwork practice at home.

SOLO VS GROUP

In conjunction with my solo practice, I like to jump in a group class every month. Although some say they go deeper during solo or online breathwork sessions because they're in the comfort of their own home, there's a mysterious energy cultivated during group sessions. The collective energy created is unique to each group that comes together. Even if you have 99 of the 100 people who were there last week, when there's just one new person, you've created an entirely new collective group energy. When you have other people breathing around you, they help raise your energy which helps you heal, and you help raise their energy which helps them heal. It's a beautiful energetic dance that happens within the invisible during group breathwork events. *T.E.A.M. = Together Everyone Achieves More!*

"Nothing in nature lives for itself. Rivers don't drink their own water. Trees don't eat their own fruit. Sun doesn't give off heat for itself. Flowers don't spread fragrance for themselves. Living for others is the rule of nature. And therein lies the secret of life."

—*Amit Gupta*

WHAT TO EXPECT

We've learned that all expectations lead to disappointment. However, if you take a look at this list of breakthroughs that people are experiencing at my breathwork events, it's fascinating to see what can happen:

- A massive release of stress
- Ability to manifest faster and more efficiently
- A new sense of clarity and deep knowing
- Expansion of consciousness and awareness (ability to see the bigger picture)
- New insights, revelations, and epiphanies (sometimes very mystical)
- Awakening to their higher purpose and mission
- A deeper connection to their higher-self and Source
- Overwhelming feelings of joy and bliss
- Deep relaxation and inner peace
- Feeling of oneness with the Universe and humanity
- Ability to quiet the monkey mind, a.k.a. "The Critic"
- Feeling of deep love for self and others never felt before

- The release of toxins and negativity from their energy field
- Profound healing from old wounds, trauma, and grief
- Release of old emotions and negative patterns
- Transcendence of self (being reborn)

I know, I know, it sounds too good to be true. So you may be asking yourself, how is this all possible just by breathing? The effects of breathwork are undeniable, and it is something that cannot be described, only experienced. You don't have to take my word for it, see what others are saying:

> *"I can't remember the last time I felt this good."*
> —Rob Harrand, Los Angeles Dodgers

> *"Breathwork is freaking powerful!"*
> —Jackie Sanchez, Health & Wellness Coach

> *"Kurtis has a unique gift, and he shares it with you by taking you on a life-changing journey. A journey inspired by breath!"*
> —Leon Logothetis,
> Star of *The Kindness Diaries* on Netflix

> *"Our in-office Breathwork session was amazing and the staff loved Kurtis. Will be sharing what you do with everyone, thank you so much. Can't wait to have you back!"*
> —Scooter Braun Projects, Management Team
> for Ariana Grande, Justin Bieber, Kanye West…

"Thank you for such a powerful night full of mind-blowing positive energy."
—Marlene Spalette, Registered Nurse

"The amount of clarity and visions I received during Kurtis' Breathwork Detox was astounding."
—Robert Angel, Creator of the popular board game Pictionary

WHICH BREATHWORK STYLE IS FOR ME?

The simple, yet long answer is to try them all like I have and see which one resonates with you the most. When I surveyed many new and experienced breathworkers, I realized they all shared similar reasons for practicing breathwork over other modalities:

1. It works best for clearing out negative energy (healing)
2. It makes them feel good (mood)
3. It provides tremendous clarity (mind state)

I couldn't agree more, and that is why I do Breathwork Detox every day, to effectively detox my mind and clear out any stored emotions or stagnant energy blocking my creativity.

WHY YOU NEED TO DETOX

"You cannot start the next chapter of your life if you keep re-reading the last one."

—Michael McMillan

They say knowledge is learning something new every day, and wisdom is letting go of something every day. As the great Master Yoda said, "You must unlearn what you have learned." The philosophies behind healing and manifesting are simple—you have to "let go" in order to "let in." They are all referring to "The Detox." You must empty your cup before you can fill it up.

We all want to take off and take flight, but similar to a plane, we cannot take off if something is blocking the runway. We need to clear the runway before we can take flight. While there are many places we would like to land, we often spin our wheels or fly in circles because there's something that needs to be cleared and removed from our life beforehand. Once that object or situation has been removed and dealt with, we can receive the clearance we need to arrive at our desired destination.

> *"The captain has turned off the seat belt sign, and you are now free to move about the cabin."*

The Universe is the command tower that can see all possible routes, flight plans, and objects on the ground and in the sky. If we are not able to land or take off, it means only one thing: something is blocking the runway and needs to be cleared first.

This is why detoxing is so powerful when it comes to manifesting anything new. We first need to remove the clutter from our lives to create the space it requires. This is why professional athletes, bodybuilders, and fitness professionals talk so much about the importance of detoxing, and why every spiritual master or guru does a major detox, cleanse, or fast before initiating a new journey.

Recalibrate, reset, rewire, restructure, reorganize, reprogram, reconfigure, reboot and recharge ... THIS is what Breathwork Detox is all about!

Below is a snippet from an amazing article I read a few years ago from a very reputable site called *Mind Body Green* discussing the 10 reasons why everyone needs to detox.

10 REASONS PEOPLE DETOX

1. Remove toxins from the body.

Long-term exposure to toxins (environmental pollutants, cancer-causing chemicals, preservatives, pesticides, heavy metals, and industrial waste) affects our metabolism, behavior, immune system, and leads to disease. They are stored in tissues and cells throughout the body, including the brain, often for years—yikes!

2. Prevent chronic disease.

Environmental toxins are responsible for many cancers, neurological diseases, heart disease, strokes… you name it. Our bodies do have a built-in detox function to deal with these dangers, but those systems are constantly overloaded! Detoxing assists and improves what our bodies are trying to do naturally.

3. Enhance immune system function.

A compromised immune system makes us vulnerable to colds and flus, affecting our quality of life and productivity. Regular detoxing helps strengthen immune system functioning and fights off infection.

4. Lose weight.

Toxins affect the body's natural ability to burn fat, leading to weight gain. Diabetes, heart disease, and high blood pressure are directly linked to weight issues. Detoxing rids the body of toxins stored in fat cells and increases metabolism.

5. Slow premature aging.

Detoxing rids the body of free radicals and heavy metals partially responsible for aging. Detoxing helps to increase nutrient absorption, including antioxidants and vitamins that help fight oxidative stress.

6. Improve the quality of life.

Simply put, our bodies don't function very well when they're loaded with toxins. We may have joint pain, headaches, digestive disorders, sleep problems, and lack of energy. Depression may be relieved and memory may be improved as a result of detoxification!

7. Increase energy.

You will have more mental, physical, and emotional energy after detoxing. People tend to sleep better and need less of it.

8. Improve skin quality.

Diet and environmental toxins undeniably affect skin. Detoxing wards off acne, strengthens hair and nails, and gives us a natural, healthy glow.

9. Mental and emotional clarity.

When the body's systems are aligned, a shift also occurs within our mental and emotional states. We can handle more when we're clear and grounded. We can make better decisions, analyze accurately, and see things differently.

10. Restore balance to our body's systems.

Our digestive, nervous, and hormonal systems were designed to work together to achieve optimum health. This is what our bodies want to do! When we overload them with toxins and unhealthy foods, these systems don't work as well as they should, and we get sick.

These are the reasons why we need to detox. Detoxing brings balance back to our systems and helps us function properly, but we need more than just a physical detox. Most of us also need a mental detox, emotional detox, and a spiritual detox. The Breathwork Detox was designed for just that. So let's start with the mind first, because it's a terrible thing to waste.

MENTAL DETOX

Several studies show that people have about 55,000 thoughts per day, and 80% of the average person's thoughts are negative in nature. 98% of their daily thoughts are the same exact thoughts they had the day before. Shocking, but sadly, not surprising.

Unfortunately, many of us are "stuck" on this hamster wheel of recycling negative thoughts that eventually turn into negative emotions. Then these negative emotions create MORE negative thoughts, which in turn feed more negative emotions, because we don't know how to get off the ride and we can't find the off switch.

BIOHACKING WITH THE BREATH

I facilitated a corporate breathwork session at Scooter Braun's company. Afterwards, a gentleman came up to me and said, "Man, the music was really loud. Is it supposed to be that loud? I could barely think!"

I laughed and replied, "GOOD! I don't *want* you to think. That's the whole point." The mind is a bad neighborhood to hang around. You may want to visit from time to time but living there can be stressful. As Tony Robbins says, "If you're in your head, you're dead." The only way to get out of your head is to get back into your body. Breathwork can be that vehicle for you! Breathwork and dancing are the two best ways to get back into your body.

Breathing has such an immediate impact on your mind and body. Many people invest in diet and exercise, but very few invest in the quality of their breath. This is a huge missed opportunity for bio-hackers and health-seekers.

One of the coolest things about breathwork is that it induces something called *Transient Hypofrontality*, also known as *flow state*. My friend Rian Doris is the CGO of Steven Kotler's Flow Research Collective and right now they are loving what breathwork is doing for *flow-hacking*.

Right around the ten- to twelve-minute mark into breathwork, the prefrontal cortex begins to quiet down. The prefrontal cortex is the executive decision maker, the part of the brain that tells us, "This is good, this is bad, you are you, and I am me." Sometimes this part of the brain is referred to as the monkey mind, the ego, or "the critic." However, it doesn't go out without putting up a fight, and a good one at that. Many people experience a lot of resistance in the beginning of breathwork, and what I noticed is the people who experience the greatest resistance are the ones who end up having the biggest breakthroughs.

The "resistance" you're breaking through during breathwork are the thoughts and mental blocks that arise. These thoughts have always been going on "behind the scene" of your awareness, but they become amplified once you wander outside your brain's comfort zone. It's like a sensor that goes off and triggers all your subconscious thoughts to surface in order to prevent you from breaking through.

This is the hardest part about breathwork. It's your brain's job to keep you safe, and when it can't scare you anymore, it tries to confuse you or distract you. Your brain thinks it's protecting you, but really it's holding you back by trying to keep you in your comfort zone. As Dr. Joe Dispenza says, "The feeling of comfort doesn't feel right, it feels familiar."

During breathwork, everyone is given two choices: push past the discomfort when it arises and move your life into accelerated growth, or retreat back into safety and comfort. When you feel uncomfortable, that means you're growing. When you begin to feel really uncomfortable during breathwork, know that a big breakthrough is on the other side of your discomfort.

Once you breathe through the discomfort and the veil of the prefrontal cortex begins to thin, something amazing happens. The resistance begins to fade and the breath almost becomes automatic. The mind becomes super-clear and an immense amount of creativity and insight pours in. Revelations occur, and you begin to solve your own problems easily and effortlessly. I've never experienced anything natural that enhances creativity like Breathwork Detox. It's by far my favorite part of breathwork and this is why I make it a daily practice. However, I don't believe breathwork enhances your creativity; instead, I believe it removes everything that's blocking you from the flow of your own creativity and cosmic consciousness. Feeling the force of creative energy run through you is possessing the energy of creation itself, which gives you the greatest power in the Universe. Creative energy is *more* than creative energy; it's healing energy and God energy, the force of creation within that's being expressed through you.

BREATHWORK IS TRIPPY!

"Inward is not a direction. Inward is a dimension."
—Jaggi Vasudev

This is the part of breathwork I call, "the spiritual detox aspect." Dr. Stan Groff, a well-known name in breathwork, specialized in substance-induced trances prior to his breathwork revelation. After LSD became illegal in the 1960s, Groff was looking for a replacement that could help his clients and patients process trauma as effectively. He soon discovered breathwork and found that it naturally helped them reach similar states. Even brain EEG studies confirmed this by showing the brain waves (theta and delta patterns) of someone doing breathwork and LSD and they were very similar. They noticed the slower waves dominated the breathing pattern. They also monitored the slow bursts of higher voltage activity which were recorded as flashbacks or emotional spikes where their brain EEG pattern changed. So you may be asking yourself, how can breathwork be just as powerful as LSD?

"The only way OUT, is IN!"

There's a gland in the human body located between our two eyebrows called the pineal gland, also known as the "third eye" in metaphysics. This tiny gland produces a substance called "DMT," dimethyltryptamine, also known as "The Spirit Molecule." This is the same psychedelic component that's in ayahuasca and the same element that fuels our dream state. When we sleep, the pineal gland secretes DMT into the brain, launching us into another dimension of adventure. The lungs actually produce more DMT than anywhere else in the body. Therefore, during breathwork, it's not uncommon to get high on your own supply. Many people experience this natural euphoric high during breathwork that can enhance their mood sometimes for days after the experience. But don't worry. A psychedelic breathwork experience isn't like LSD, ayahuasca, or magic mushrooms, where once you commit to psychedelic plant medicine you're stuck on that ride for a few hours (whether you like it or not). Breathwork is different because YOU ARE IN CHARGE. You can speed up the ride or slow it down as you choose, or even stop it completely. The choice is yours. At any time you can pull the ripcord and hit the eject button by stopping the active mouth-breathing and switching to nostril breathing. This reverses and slows the process. A lot of times people stop or slow down due to fear. Just remember: to have a breakthrough, YOU MUST BREAK THROUGH!

If you want to cut down a tree and never have it grow back, you don't cut off the leaves and the branches but allow the trunk to remain. You would cut down the entire tree and rip out the roots. That is the philosophy of healing trauma through Breathwork Detox, which is getting to "the root of the problem." If you want to have a breakthrough and get to the root of your problems, this next chapter is for you. This is where the magic lives! It's the treasure chest we've been looking for; just like any diamond, jewel, or gem, we must dig deep to find it.

EMOTIONAL DETOX

"Sometimes the weight you need to lose isn't on your body."

—Unknown

We hold stress, anxiety, depression, and grief in our lungs and chest. The subclavicular area (the area beneath the clavicle or collarbone) is where we store the fear of death. We tend to store a lot of fear in the scalenes (upper chest/collarbone area). The throat is the first thing to close up when we experience powerful emotions. The scalenes hold the screams we don't scream, all the energy we stored from biting our tongue and not speaking up when we should have. We also store a lot of childhood memories in the chest and upper diaphragm. This is why we first breathe into the belly, then into the chest, to clear out these emotional storage centers all at once.

"You gotta feel it to heal it."

Emotions are energy-in-motion. When these energies (emotions) aren't fully expressed outwardly, they clog the *nadis* and meridians (energy channels) and are stuck in the body. Knowing that energy isn't created nor destroyed, when we hold back our tears, where do you think that energy goes? That energy and emotion is pushed into the cells of your body until another issue arises where it can be expressed again and hopefully released. If that emotion isn't expressed quickly and stays suppressed instead, it begins to build and congest inside your energy channels which can turn into disease or illness. Remember, the issues are in the tissues!

"The mind tends to live in the future. The body holds onto things from the past, and the soul keeps us anchored in the present."

—Kurtis Lee Thomas

The cellular memory of the body is subconscious; it is all-knowing. It never lies nor forgets, and most importantly, it keeps score! When we experienced some form of trauma as children, we didn't have the emotional intelligence at the time to process that trauma. So we took that energy, that experience, and stored it somewhere in the body so we could deal with it later. We ran into trouble when more and more external conflict compounded over the years, creating layers of suppression. These energies must be dealt with before the lid blows, because we have a finite capacity for what we can handle.

Unfortunately pills don't fix the issue; they only suppress it deeper and we don't want to suppress them any more than we already have. Better OUT than IN! If we don't make conscious choices and do something about it now, we could end up with serious mental and physical health issues like what I experienced. This is what Freud meant when he famously stated, *"Unexpressed emotions will never die. They are buried alive and come forth in uglier ways."*

Often we store these emotionally-charged energies in our stomach or hips. If you were to move really close to someone (invade their space) and enter their "bubble," you would see the first area of the body they protect and try to cover is their stomach. The belly is where we hide these emotions; it's our vulnerable space. Similarly, when people become sad or depressed, the first areas they gain weight are in and around the stomach and the hips. On a subconscious level, we use the fat as a protection mechanism to hide these suppressed emotions from others, because we don't want anyone to see our vulnerability. This is also why so many don't breathe correctly into their diaphragm and actually avoid deep belly breathing. We constrict breathing into our belly because subconsciously we believe the less we breathe, the less we will feel. However, this not only prevents the full expression of pain but prevents all the pleasurable feelings that life offers.

BREATHWORK AND HEART HEALTH

"The breath is the guardian to the heart. There's a reason why your lungs are wrapped around your heart.... every breath is a prayer, every breath is a blessing."

—Dan Brulé

Your breathing rate and your heart rate are tied together in a phenomenon called "respiratory sinus arrhythmia (RSA)." When you inhale, your heart rate increases slightly and then decreases again when you exhale. This is why the breath is so effective in controlling bodily functions and autonomic stress responses. Dr. David O'Hare wrote a book called *Heart coherence 365*. It's a therapeutic practice based on rhythmic breathing that's recognized by the scientific world and recommended by doctors. 365 represents the breathing technique of 3 times a day, 6 breaths a minute, for 5 minutes.

How are you breathing right now? Is your heart beat relaxed? Or is it stressed? Your HRV would be a good indication. HRV stands for Heart Rate Variability. HRV isn't the amount of heartbeats we have. It's the harmony and measure of the space between each beat. To simplify it, higher HRV is good, and low HRV is bad. Research shows there's a relationship between low HRV and increased anxiety and depression. Low HRV is also linked to increased risk of death and car-diovascular disease.

Breathwork raises your HRV. Why is this important? Because higher HRV makes you more resilient to stress and improves cardiovascular performance. Diaphragmatic breathing (breathwork) massages the vagus nerve and reduces stress while lowering heart rate and blood pressure. When our heartbeat is relaxed, we are in our parasympathetic nervous system (rest and digestion). When our heartbeat is stressed, we're in our sympathetic nervous system (fight or flight).

WEIGHT LOSS WITH BREATHWORK

Everyone at some point in their life has been on some kind of diet or detox. Little did we know that our lungs remove 70% of the toxins in the body. Oxygen also plays a crucial role in burning fat because oxygen helps break down the fat molecules and the waste (carbon dioxide) exits the body via the lungs. Carbon dioxide is heavy; we breathe out about a pound of it everyday. Therefore, the more oxygen we take in, the more fat molecules we are able to burn off. There is no other practice out there that takes more oxygen into the body than breathwork.

> *"Human energy comes from food and oxygen, but food only gives us 10 percent of our energy needs. Oxygen is required for the other 90 percent of our energy, and every cell in the body requires oxygen to live."*
>
> —Sciencing.com

Breath is the primary delivery system for electricity and energy in the body. When we inhale, we absorb oxygen into the lungs that immediately goes to our bloodstream and into every cell in our being. Lack of oxygen and increased tension in the body hinders the flow of blood, nutrients, and vital energy which can cause insomnia and chronic fatigue. In other words, you can buy all the expensive supplements and organic-vegan food you want, but if you're not breathing correctly, you will not reap the benefits of all the good food and vitamins you're splurging on. In addition, when the body is oxygen-deprived, bacteria and viruses thrive. Many people are only taking in 20-30% of their lung capacity and starving their cells from oxygen and vital life force energy. Conscious breathing is a completely untapped superpower, that when used intently, can transform our lives.

In addition, when you begin to practice breathwork, your diaphragm and abdominal wall stretches and strengthens, which increases the blood circulation and flow of prana/chi in the belly. This bioenergetic motility increases the peristalsis[3] in the stomach which creates better digestion, nutrient absorption, and elimination of toxins. That's the reason so many people experience weight loss while on the Breathwork Detox program.

A major yet unspoken area of weight gain that's rarely discussed is "emotional eating." Harvard researchers have reported that stress from work and other areas correlates with weight gain. Stress also seems to affect our food preferences. When we're stressed, the adrenal glands release a hormone called cortisol which increases our appetite. That hormone tends to crave sugary and fatty foods more than healthy ones.

> *"There is much truth behind the phrase 'stress eating.' Stress, the hormones it unleashes, and the effects of high-fat, sugary 'comfort' foods, that push people toward overeating."*
> —Harvard Health Publishing (health.harvard.edu)

---

3 *Peristalsis* is "the involuntary constriction and relaxation of the muscles of the intestine or another canal, creating wave-like movements that push the contents of the canal forward." Lexico, Oxford's Dictionary Online, https://www.lexico.com/en/definition/peristalsis

Breathwork is so effective in weight loss because it helps eradicate the chronic stress and anxiety that lead to stress-eating and worse conditions. The great thing about breathwork is that it gets to the root cause of these emotional imbalances and helps clear those blockages out of the body that can wreak havoc if gone unchecked.

DUMP THE EMOTIONAL BAGGAGE

Unresolved emotions from the past, unhealthy beliefs, and negative thought patterns sabotage our current joy and drain our life force energy. This is what many refer to as "baggage," which is something we ALL carry with us and bring into our current relationships (personal and professional).

Over the years, we accumulate many emotional traumas, stresses, failures, rejections, heartbreaks, and financial burdens that ultimately create "unconscious" habits that bleed into our daily lives. Breathwork helps us "let go" and finally get rid of the emotional baggage we're not even aware we've been carrying. These energies are the culprits that have been preventing us from manifesting what we want and experiencing the emotions we want out of life.

Trapped emotions and repressed feelings increase cortisol levels and lower our immune system. By releasing these stagnant energies within the body, the breathwork process can help ignite a landslide of clearing and healing that is particularly effective with the following:

- Stress
- Anxiety
- Depression

- Lethargy/fatigue
- Emotional detox
- Weight loss
- Balancing the nervous system
- Pain management
- Creativity
- Divine messages/epiphanies
- Increased energy levels
- Enhanced consciousness
- Trauma/emotional release

According to Louise Hay's international best-selling book, *You Can Heal Your Life*, which sold over 30 million copies, heavy emotions like depression and grief are stored in the lungs. She states that the lungs represent the ability to take life in, and when we have feelings of unworthiness and not living life fully, we begin to have dysfunction in our lungs and breathing. She also says, "Asthma represents the inability to breathe for one's self; feeling stifled; and suppressed crying." I highly recommend this book because it shows the correlation between emotions and certain areas of the body. It also gives the affirmation we need to change the belief system that may have caused that issue in the first place. It links all conditions, whether we're dealing with acne, back pain, shoulder pain, or even prostate cancer.

People sometimes wonder how a billionaire like Steve Jobs, with all the money and resources in the world, could die of cancer. Well here's the thing: it doesn't matter how much money you have or have many green juices you drink, if you have suppressed trauma or you're carrying around the burdens of guilt, shame, regret, or anger, it's a death wish!

Woody Harrleson said, *"I don't get mad, I grow a tumor."* Sigmund Freud stated, *"Unexpressed emotions will never die. They are buried alive and will come forth in uglier ways."* If we don't allow ourselves to feel the scary emotions we need to feel, that energy stays in the body like poison. If we don't clear out those toxic emotions and reverse the core belief that caused the illness, it's very hard to heal. If we don't express ourselves, speak our mind, forgive ourselves, or forgive others by saying, "I'm sorry," or "I love you," those burdens will haunt us for the rest of our lives. We have to clear these energies out by any and all means necessary.

> *"What NOT to say to someone with anxiety or depression: 'Just get over it,' 'Stop worrying,' 'You're just overthinking,' 'Snap out of it,' 'Relax,' 'It's not a big deal.'"*
> —Alison Seponara, @TheAnxietyHealer

Affirmations are highly effective when used during or after breathwork since breathwork induces a hypnotic state where the neuroplasticity of the brain is highly suggestible. I use an amazing app called "ThinkUp," where I can record affirmations in my own voice over meditation music. I then listen to the recordings with headphones while I sleep, with the volume so low that my conscious mind can barely hear what I'm saying. This is highly effective, because the conscious mind doesn't need to hear what's being said if the subconscious is hearing it. If you are struggling with some form of S.A.D., here are 20 inspirational affirmations that Louise Hay recommends to help you heal from stress, anxiety, and depression:

- I trust the process of life.
- All is well in my world. Everything is working out for my highest good. Out of this situation only good will come. I am safe!
- I am at home in my body.
- I forgive myself and set myself free.
- I love and approve of myself.
- I deserve all that is good.
- It is safe for me to speak up for myself.
- I forgive everyone in my past for all perceived wrongs. I release them with love.
- I do not have to prove myself to anyone.
- I trust my intuition. I am willing to listen to that still, small voice within.
- I welcome miracles into my life.
- I am in the process of positive change.
- Whatever I need to know is revealed to me at exactly the right time.
- Deep at the center of my being is an infinite well of love.
- I am loved, and I am at peace.
- I am Divinely guided and protected at all times.
- I listen with love to my body's messages.
- I forgive myself for not being perfect.

FAMILY MATTERS

As if we didn't have enough trauma of our own, studies show that as children, we adopt our parents beliefs, fears, and traumas, some even before we're born. One of these studies was cited in the book, *The Quantum Mindset in a Nutshell* by Rick Thompson: "Among the tens of thousands of people who were directly exposed to the 9/11 terrorist attack were approximately 1,700 pregnant women. Many of these women developed symptoms of PTSD, and some of their children inherited the trauma that their mothers experienced on that horrific day. Some transferred trauma to their unborn children, and their babies were born with noticeably higher cortisol levels than normal."

Generational trauma is a real thing and science agrees. I'd like to refer to a study I read in the *Washington Post* by journalist Meeri Kim:

> In the experiment, researchers taught male mice to fear the smell of cherry blossoms by associating the scent with mild foot shocks. Two weeks later, they bred with females. The resulting mice pups were raised to adulthood having never been exposed to the smell. Yet when the critters caught a whiff of it for the first time, they suddenly became anxious and fearful. They were even born with more cherry-blossom-detecting neurons in their noses and more brain space devoted to cherry-blossom-smelling. The memory transmission extended out another generation when these male mice bred, and similar results were found. Neuroscientists at Emory University found that genetic markers, thought to be wiped clean before birth, were used to transmit a single traumatic experience across generations, leaving behind traces in the behavior and anatomy of future pups.

These 9/11 babies and newborn mice were born innocent to the world around them, yet they harbor generations worth of information, both bad and good, passed down by their ancestors.

When we heal ourselves, we heal entire generations. We are all intimately connected to one another beyond space, time, and even throughout lifetimes.

CRY BABIES

"The first thing we do when we are born is we breathe in, and we cry. And the last thing we do is breathe out, and other people cry."
—Paraphrased from *Management Mantras*
by Sri Sri Ravi Shankar

Crying is the best way to clear out trauma from your energy field. Holding in your tears is one of the worst things you can do for yourself. When we cry, it's a gift; crying is a HUGE emotional release for the body. Unfortunately, men think they'll be less of a man if they cry.

Crying is very liberating! Once I released a painful memory during breathwork, but I was crying tears of joy because I was so grateful I could release the hurt I had been holding onto for so long.

Another amazing way to release emotional build up and stagnant energies is by shaking and twitching. I know it sounds crazy, but it's true and it works very well. There's a healing modality called TRE (Trauma Release Exercises) that recommends tremors and shaking, because this is the body's natural mechanism to release trauma. If you've ever seen a gazelle or zebra escape after being chased by a lion, the first thing they do is shake. This shaking is a protection mechanism that allows the trauma and anxiety to leave the body so it isn't stored in their tissues to wreak havoc later.

ANXIETY AND BREATHWORK

urprisingly, many people are timid of group breathwork because they believe they are empathic or "sensitive" to energies. This may be the case for some, but most people who feel they're empaths are just hyper-reactive, not hyper-sensitive. In other words, their senses are overloaded due to the amount of anxiety they have that needs to be purged. Their body begins to overreact to all the outside stimuli of the world. Instead of being receptive to other people's energies, the opposite happens. Their energy field rejects it and this disharmony results in anxiety or sensory overload when they're around large groups. I noticed that after a few breathwork detox sessions, these same people don't have such a challenge anymore, even if they've had it for years, or their entire lifetime.

Breathwork techniques are also great for helping alleviate the fear of public speaking, chronic worrying, and overwhelm. However, there is a very thin line between anxiety and excitement. Both speed up the heart beat, increase cortisol, and prepare the body for action. Anxiety is a signal for arousal and we must learn to reframe this energy to work *for* us instead of against us. We can communicate this message to the brain by breathing and using affirmations; this halts the anxiety as we improve our ability to reframe the energy.

Alison Wood Brooks, a professor at Harvard Business School, is an expert on this phenomenon and coined it "anxious reappraisal." Her studies show there's a thin line between fear and excitement. When you're anxious, it's easier to convince yourself to be excited than to be calm.

Alison recommends making a list of all the ways the "anxiety-inducing events" can go well, and how they may benefit you and change your life for the better.

Personally, what helps me when I can't find a way to make myself calm or to get excited is to stop, drop, and do about ten minutes of breathwork. This clears excess stress and anxious energy and helps neutralize overactive thoughts.

BREATH AWARENESS

You've probably heard this one before: "Be more aware of your thoughts." The problem is that we have over 55,000 thoughts per day. Trying to corral all our crazy thoughts can be a mess; however, tuning into our breath is much easier. Forget about trying to be aware of all your thoughts, all the time. We want to get away from practices that keep us in the mind; we want to live in our body. Plus, it's much more effective to pay attention to the body and be aware of how we're feeling. Our emotions are indications of what we're thinking, because our emotions are the manifestation of our thoughts. Instead of trying to change your thoughts, first check in with your breathing.

BREATH WATCHING

Breath Watching is a meditation; it's the observation of your breath. You are <u>not</u> consciously breathing. You simply watch, feel, and observe the breath. That's all. You focus on the sensations of the breath, the rising and falling, and the sensation of the air passing through your nose or mouth. When the mind (awareness) wanders, just bring that awareness back to the breath. Ten to twenty minutes of breath watching per day is a solid meditation practice. Breath awareness is one of the most powerful hacks for expanding awareness and consciousness. It's one of the greatest spiritual training exercises you can do, wherever and whenever.

"The mind and the breath are the king and queen of human consciousness."

—Leonard D. Orr

How are you breathing right now? When's the last time you "checked in?"

As the illustrious saying goes, "Know thyself." Conscious breathing raises consciousness. When you become more aware of your breathing, you suddenly become aware of your posture and other subtle energies around you. Breath awareness and posture adjustment are practices worth practicing.

Studies show that when participants assumed superhero poses for just two minutes, they positively affected their cortisol and testosterone levels and felt more confident and powerful. Even tiny adjustments in posture and alignment send messages to the brain and the nervous system about how we should feel with each posture.

Famous Yogi Sadhguru has some excellent YouTube videos showing how practicing posture can help bring a yogi to enlightenment. He states, "When the body and the spine are aligned, all the information in the Universe is available to them if they so choose."

Research supports that simply shifting your breathing pattern can influence the quality of emotions that you experience. When you consciously shift your posture or your breathing, you automatically change your emotional state. That's the power of the breath!

BREATH MIRRORING

Mirroring someone's breath can strengthen rapport with that person, just like posture and body language. Mirroring your partner's breath during love-making enhances intimacy and allows for a deeper connection. From professional sports to love-making, when we are synchronized, we think alike, react alike, and our bonds strengthen, allowing for better performance and an overall better human experience.

RING THE ALARM

Bells and alarms set off triggers in our mind that communicate to our sympathetic nervous system. We hear these warning sounds on a daily basis, whether it's our alarm clock in the morning or a fire alarm in school. We were all programmed to run and scatter to our next class when we heard the bell ring to avoid being late. But what if we were programmed to do something else when we heard a bell ring? I read about a school that implemented a new "alarm system" with their teachers and students. Whenever the bell would ring, instead of racing out of the room, they would sit peacefully for a moment and do a "reset" using transitional meditation, a.k.a transitional breathing. This short exercise would give them a soft reset before going to their next class.

STOP, DROP, AND BREATHE!
(BREATH RESETS)

Even taking just one deep breath before you switch tasks can make a significant difference in your life. You could do this before going to the bathroom, making some food, calling someone, answering the phone, or before leaving the house. Studies show that disorganized people usually get lost in transition. They can focus while they're doing something, but the moment they get up to do something else, get a call, or somehow get interrupted, they forget what they were doing before. Napoleon Hill called these people "drifters."

We all do it though. We get lost and distracted while transitioning through our daily tasks. As soon as the mind unlocks from one task, it goes back to wandering and drifting and we are lost in the sea of the abyss. It's difficult to do deep work if we allow ourselves to get lost in the transitions, which happens much more frequently than we realize. When we learn to manage our transitions, we train ourselves to be more focused and organized. Therefore, practicing the art of "re-focusing" is a skill worth mastering.

The purpose of breath resets, or transitional breathing, is to learn how to become conscious during our transitions. It also helps us not to carry one "energy residue" over to the next when switching tasks. In other words, we shouldn't take the energy from the phone call with our boss to the email to our grandmother. We do this all the time without even realizing it. The practice of shifting helps us find our reset button. Some people do this by closing their eyes and taking one or two deep conscious breaths. Others close their eyes for one to three minutes while repeating the words "release tension everywhere." Then they set their intention for what they want to feel and accomplish next. Brendon Burchard has a good video on YouTube about RMT (Release Meditation Technique).

Many people who smoke cigarettes say they feel calm and relaxed afterward. In fact, the 2,000 chemicals they're inhaling are entering their bloodstream and stimulating their nervous system in a very toxic and erratic way that affects their mental and emotional state and sleep habits. The real reason they feel this sense of relief is because they're taking a short break away from life and focusing on their breathing for 10-15 minutes. Inadvertently, they've adopted a breathing exercise that triggers their parasympathetic nervous system because they're exhaling more than they're inhaling. Unfortunately, smoking doesn't calm our emotions; it suppresses them. People who don't have the tools to manage their anxiety tend to smoke just to cope when the body is under massive stress.

A study conducted by the Center of Tobacco Research and Intervention with the University of Wisconsin School of Medicine and Public Health reported that 50% of the soldiers who went to war would come back addicted to tobacco. I believe if these soldiers had been given breathwork techniques, it would have not only saved them from addiction and poor health, but it would have helped them release massive emotional stress and trauma that could eventually lead to PTSD. We lose 20 veterans per day to suicide, but the good news is that now the Department of Defense is advocating breathwork for veterans, and for very good reasons.

It's never effective to try to get someone to quit doing something they're addicted to, because everyone is trying to get them to quit. They become reactive. Sometimes what we resist, persists, and what we fight, we ignite! However, if you can get them to breathe and do the things that make them feel good, they'll want to quit themselves. An example of how this works was best explained in a dialogue between student and teacher in the documentary, *Autobiography of a Yogi:*

Yogananda: Do you smoke?

Student: Yes.

Yogananda: You may continue. Do you drink alcohol?

Student: Yes.

Yogananda: You may continue. Do you enjoy the opposite sex promiscuously?

Student: Yes

Yogananda: Well, you may continue!

Student: Wait a minute. You mean, I can come up on this hill ... with all these wonderful people ... and study these teachings, and I can go back down there and do all these things?

Yogananda: Absolutely! But I will not promise you that as you continue to study these teachings that the desire to do these things won't fall away from you.

If people can take cigarette breaks just to suck down poison every two hours, I'm sure they can take a few breath-breaks every day as well. Breath-resets and this next exercise are extremely powerful tools that are easy to do and highly effective (my favorite).

WHERE ATTENTION GOES, ENERGY FLOWS!

One of my favorite exercises is the simplest and most over-looked breathing technique of them all. It can be used as a breath-reset or an instant stress reliever. It's the one breath-ing exercise I do the most out of all of them, and it's called "the sigh." Even famous breathwork teacher Dan Brulé emphasizes that within 30 years of teaching breathwork, "the sigh" was the greatest breath-hack that he discovered. We usually sigh as an unconscious habit, but what is a sigh and why do we do it?

The body sighs to relieve itself from stress and pain. The moment the body releases these heavy energies, we hear a "sigh of relief." When you consciously sigh, you are sending messages to release stress and pain from the body. This is such an amazing breath-hack; I can't emphasize how effec-tive it is. You should do this exercise as much and as often as you can.

This is how I have fun with this exercise. When I'm tuning into my body, I ask myself, "Where do I feel discomfort or pain?" I immediately focus all my energy on that area and breathe into where I feel that discomfort (in through the nose or mouth). When all the air in that area is filled with conscious breath, I let out a big loud, obnoxious, and over-exaggerated sigh through my mouth. The areas I focus on are the areas where I store lots of energy, typically behind the navel, the heart, the solar plexus, or wherever I feel even the slightest discomfort.

This practice is really the practice of body awareness and letting go. The more you practice this technique, the more conscious you will become and the better you will get at *letting go* because everything in life is connected to everything else. The exhale in the sigh is the same exhale we use in Breathwork Detox. It should only be 1-2 seconds long no matter how much or how little you inhale, because the exhale will always be the same. If it takes you longer than 1 or 2 seconds to release the exhale, chances are you are holding onto something else besides the breath.

As they say, "let go or get dragged." When you let go of this breath, relax the jaw completely and let something else go with it. There is a skill to master when it comes to releasing the exhale because what we are really mastering is the art of *letting go*. Letting go of the exhale should be effortless; it's an act of surrender. Similar to pulling back an arrow in archery, you already did all the hard work with the inhale. The exhale should simply be the release of the inhale the same as you would release the arrow from the bow after drawing it back. We're not meant to hold onto things; this is why the body gets shaky when we try. If you find it difficult to let go of your breath, you're probably struggling with letting go of the things holding you back in life: failures, anger, regret, guilt, shame, and doubt. When you learn to release and empty yourself, you don't lose who you are; you're getting rid of everything you're not.

"Empty your cup so that it may be filled; become devoid to gain totality."

—Bruce Lee

The sigh exercise is also good to use when you notice your energy shifting, when hearing bad news, or if your thoughts begin to turn negative. As soon as you notice this, ask yourself, "Where does that thought live?" "Where does that feeling live?" Then immediately SIGH IT OUT before it triggers the mind and the body responds with the feeling of anxiousness. By doing this, you train the mind and body to use the breath instead of responding with its normal automatic stress indicators.

The prana and chi in the breath is so healing. When you consciously breathe this energy into every cell of your being, you initiate a new relationship with your body and your energy.

WHAT'S YOUR BREATH TEACHING YOU?

(BREATH ANALYSIS)

"Flexible body, flexible mind."

A quote that changed how I live my life was by T. Harv Eker: "How you do anything is how you do everything." Everything we do is connected to everything else we do; not one thing is separate from another. You can tell a lot about yourself by how you breathe. Our breathing patterns can also relate to our personality and beliefs. If your breath flows, then your life glows!

If our chest is tight, we are more likely to be uptight. When our breathing is strong and deep, we are living a more deep and meaningful life. The body is a reflection of what's going on in our mind. When we catch ourselves holding our breath, this is a slow form of suffocation, a form of self-suffering and self-sabotage.

"Resistance to breathing is resistance to change. Resistance to change is resistance to living."
—Max Strom, *A Life Worth Breathing*

My breathing workshops usually have around 100 people in them, and it's interesting to see how everyone breathes differently. The truth is, we're all experiencing some type of dysfunctional breathing. Breathwork is unique for everyone and affects everyone differently. The commonality is that it guarantees some type of shift. Which type of shift depends on what you're going through.

Breath is life! How we breathe and how we live are interconnected. Below are some examples of this interconnection. I've used unique names for entertainment purposes only.

TIMID BREATHERS: When we are shallow breathing, we are living a much more shallow life than we should. When we are breathing shallow and fast, something in life is too intense for us. These types of breathers are usually overwhelmed and stressed and can only take on small bites of life.

Students who take in very small breaths but make giant noises while exhaling are most likely going through something in life that intimidates them. This is usually a deep-seated fear or doubt about moving forward and taking that next step.

Scientifically speaking, light is information and energy. The breath channels prana/chi (light) and allows us to take in more information and energy. When we inhale, we take in information that enhances our intuition. The reason these types of breathers are only taking small breaths is because they are already overwhelmed with life and subconsciously they believe they don't need any additional information.

PITBULL BREATHERS: These types of breathers do the opposite of TIMID BREATHERS. They breathe in quickly, because they are trying to take in as much information as possible. They wish to go further and faster but something is holding them back. These types of breathers take in big inhales, yet on the exhale they close their lips and release very slowly, holding back. Pitbull breathers are ready for that next step in life, ready to take on the world, but they just can't seem to let go of the past. Subconsciously, something from their past is haunting them and preventing them from moving forward. There's something or someone they just haven't dealt with yet. They are ready for the next chapter in their life but need to stop re-reading the previous chapter and close it. Sometimes this has to do with forgiveness or just coming to terms with something. Life can be very frustrating for these types of people. It can seem as if their life is a treadmill, like they know where they want to go but just can't seem to get there. It is common for these types of breathers to go through life feeling like they have one foot on the gas and one foot on the brake.

Breathwork Detox works well for this group because this is the exact purpose of the breathwork detox. We need to clear the path so we can take off! To land at our destination, the runway must be clear. The same way we must empty our cup before we fill it, we LET GO so we can LET IN.

FLOATERS: When we experience trauma, two things can happen: 1. We store that trauma in the body, or 2. aspects of ourselves leave the body for protection. This is why shamans have a technique called "Soul Retrieval." Pieces of yourself leave so they are not energetically harmed from that experience. We must retrieve those aspects back into the body. During breathwork, I see students astral project out of their body and come back re-energized. When this happens, the soul recalibrates itself.

HEART-CENTERED: These types of breathers breathe into the chest but not into their belly. These people are givers and generally have an open heart but a weaker will. Character traits will tend to make it harder for them to say no when someone wants something from them, which causes them to be taken advantage of often. They tend to bite their tongue instead of speaking up and won't stand up for themselves when they should.

BUDDHA BELLIES: These types of breathers breathe into the belly but not as well into the chest. They tend to be strong-willed, very grounded and centered but emotionally guarded and closed off.

BREATH HOLDERS: While people who hyperventilate are more likely to flee in a "fight or flight" situation, people who tend to hold their breath are more likely to "freeze" in these situations.

People who hold their breath tend to "hide" from life. Often they're people who have experienced some type of trauma from early years. They're also more likely to have PTSD, because those emotions become trapped somewhere in the body. Breathwork for these types of people is very effective. I had a colleague who was facilitating breathwork, and in his class a guy started running "while lying on his mat." Later he learned the man was a war vet who froze in battle when bullets were flying and bombs were going off around him. He even watched his friend die in front of him. This trauma caused him to freeze and lock that memory in his body. He started running during breathwork because the body finally released the trapped emotion by responding to that trauma when it felt safe. He healed his PTSD.

OVERACHIEVERS: People who breathe with their back and shoulders instead of their diaphragm during breathwork are usually working harder than they need to work in life. I call these people ducks. Ducks just cruise across the pond ever so gently, yet if you could see them underwater, you would see that duck pedaling its little tail off like cartoon feet.

These types of people need more yin than yang in their life, more "being" than doing, more centering of their mind, body, and spirit rather than getting out there and pounding the pavement even more. They're overachievers, ready to take on the world, but they have a tough time delegating and they run the risk of burnout.

SAFETIES: These types of breathers are the ones who play everything safe. They may be willing to try new things, but they always enter with extreme caution and skepticism. These types of breathers rarely travel outside their comfort zone. No matter how much motivation I give them to keep going, they start slowly, breathe slowly, and end slowly.

These breathers tend to have a nice euphoric high after breathwork but rarely do they have massive breakthroughs.

BURN-OUTS: We can also call these people "quitters," which is such a loaded word, but let's use it anyway. Burn-outs tend to start off strong in breathwork but give up shortly after. As soon as the "mind-frick" from the monkey-mind begins to kick in, they listen to it and begin to slow down, pause, or even stop the detox breathing. Stopping the breathwork before the transient hypofrontality is like going to college and deciding not to get your diploma. These types of people usually rev their engine loudly at the start of the race, but they fizzle out and can't cross the finish line.

"If a task is once begun, never leave it 'till it's done.
Be the labor great or small, do it well or not at all."
—Author Unknown

PROCRASTINATORS: These types of breathers start off slow and sometimes listen or peek to see how others are breathing around them before really getting into it. We can be nice and call them "observers" for now. However, with breathwork, you want to rev your engine and start strong in the beginning to get the prana and chi circulating so the magic can happen. It's better to boil the water and let it simmer later, because it's much harder to pick up the pace than slow it down while detox-breathing.

"Some people make things happen. Some people
watch things happen. And then there are those who
wonder, 'What the hell just happened?'"
—Carroll Bryant

FITNESS FREAKS: You would think the fitness freaks with ripped abs would come to breathwork and kick ass. Although their willpower is strong and they're able to power through a class, sometimes their breathing sucks. Six pack abs actually restrict diaphragmatic breathing (pranayama/breathwork). Excessive tightness in that region does not allow the diaphragm to push down to fill the lungs with air. When the stomach and ribs can't expand correctly, neither can the diaphragm and lungs. Core stability is everything when it comes to physical strength and mobility. However, six pack abs and core stability aren't synonymous. You can have six pack abs without core stability.

You can actually strengthen your abs with breathwork and use your lungs to strengthen your core. The Joe Rogan Experience podcast has a good episode about this with surfer Laird Hamilton.

The bottom line is that none of the aforementioned breathing types are right, and none are wrong. They're all acceptable and have nothing to do with the experience one has during breathwork. People come to my events and I can tell just by their energy that someone dragged them there. When they're breathing, I can see them start slow, burn out, then hold their breath. In the back of my mind, I'm thinking, "Ok. Breathwork is just not for them." Then, to my complete and utter surprise, they approach me after class and tell me they had the greatest experience of their life. This has happened in my class so many times that I realized you just can't judge someone's breathing, no matter what. Breathwork just works! It's unexplainable and will work its magic on you just the way it's meant to.

BREATHWORK CAN SAVE YOUR LIFE

"Not only do we use the same breath to warm our hands and to cool off our soup, but breathing affects every organ, system, and function in the body. Every physiological, psychological, and emotional state has its own breathing pattern, and when you change one you change the other. If we can muster up the right breath at the right time, we have the cheat codes to life."

—Dan Brulé

Physiological evidence shows that implementing just one breathing practice in your everyday life can significantly reduce blood pressure and offer stress relieving benefits. Understanding how and when to use the correct breath takes practice. To help with this, I post breathing exercises on my Instagram page (@ManFromTheStars) for people to learn and practice what techniques to use for a variety of life events: business meetings, interviews, ways to relieve stress, anger, and the best breathing techniques to increase energy or enhance sleep.

I share other breathing techniques such as Tummo Breathing, Progressive Relaxation Breathing, Lamaze Breathing, Tactical Box Breathing (Square Breathing), Vertical Breathing, Band Breathing, Heart Breathing, Relaxation Breathing, Straw Breathing, Bag Breathing, Shaman's Breath, Lion's Breath, Breath of Fire, Sitali Cooling Breath (TACO Breath), Sex Breathing, Burst Breathing, Triangle Breathing, Reflexive Breathing, Shower Breath, Apnea Breathing, Ocean Breath, Resistance Breathing, and Warrior's Breath, just to name a few.

If you can master Breathwork Detox, you can master the rest of them more easily. I will give you one breathing exercise right now because this is the breath hack that literally saved my life.

LIVING THE DREAM

This timeline takes place over a decade ago. At the time, I was a celebrity jeweler who knew absolutely nothing about jewelry, but I knew how to sell products I believed in. My friend was a master jeweler for over 30 years and made some of the most elegant timepieces I've ever seen. Since he wasn't good at sales and marketing and that was my strength, he brought me on board with his company to help grow his brand. In just a month's time, we were setting up booths and gifting suites at all the big awards shows: MTV,

BET, Oscars, Grammys, and ESPYS. Life was good! I had a $50,000 timepiece on my wrist, I was driving a nice Range Rover, I had a nice home, and I had lots of cash in my pocket. Little did I know that all of this was about to change in the blink of an eye, as I experienced a great contrast of life events in a very short time period.

While doing an ESPY event at the Playboy Mansion, thinking I was "living it up," I received a phone call from the police department asking me where I was. I asked, "Why?"

They said, "Because your house is burning down!"

My jaw dropped, and a million thoughts came flooding in. I began to panic. Things started to turn south for me. My life started to fall apart, like dominos falling, one by one.

Not long after this phone call, my productivity began to decline. I lost my job, I ran out of money, and had to sell my truck to pay my bills. Just when I thought it couldn't get any worse, I woke up to an early morning call from my father telling me that my brother and his girlfriend had been shot and killed in an armed robbery at their home. Needless to say, I was devastated!

My anxiety began to build, unbeknownst to me. Out of nowhere, I began to have something I had always heard about but never fully understood, until now... panic attacks!

WORSE THAN DEATH

I've been on an airplane that was preparing for a crash landing. My friends and I lifted a car on the highway that was flipped over and saved two girls from being crushed. I felt bullets fly by my head in a nightclub after shots were fired. I saw someone shot in front of me and a friend and I had to take them to the emergency room. I've been on vacation and had to have emergency surgery in a foreign place. But let me tell you, nothing is scarier than a panic attack. You literally feel like you're dying. I'm sure death is much faster and easier than feeling like your heart, mind, and body are about to collapse or explode. For anyone out there who had or is currently experiencing panic attacks, I have so much compassion for what you are going through. Let me share what eradicated mine and what I believe saved my life.

DISABLED BY ANXIETY

During this time of despair, I had been coping by taking anti-depressants and anti-anxiety medication. Whenever I would feel a panic attack come on, I would snatch the bottle of pills that I took with me everywhere I went and would immediately take one. More panic attacks started to surface, and soon I doubled the dose. Soon after, I tripled the dose because the panic attacks were getting worse and were coming more frequently. They were so bad I couldn't work, and I had to move into my mother's basement. I had a bell on my nightstand that I would grab and ring vigorously when I started to have a panic attack. My mother would hear the bell and come down to comfort me. I couldn't scream for her help, because my throat would close up on me. Imagine what it was like, being a grown man and having to go through something like this. I felt helpless, pathetic, and embarrassed. I was disabled by my anxiety.

One day I went to my doctor's office for a follow up, but my primary doctor wasn't there that day. A female Asian doctor was filling in, who asked lots of questions. I shared everything I was doing and going through. I remember her distinctly saying, "Kurtis, if you keep taking those anti-anxiety pills like you are, you are heading down a dark path of no return." She told me that I was the one triggering the panic attacks by simply making the decision to take the pill which I believed would get rid of the panic attack. In fact, it was causing it. (I'm not sure if you just caught that, because it didn't make sense when she first told me either.)

She advised me to get off the anti-anxiety meds but to stay on the antidepressants <u>for no longer than 3 months MAX</u>, while weaning off them the last two to three weeks. She said this would reset my system and regulate my emotional highs and lows. She strongly advised to immediately stop taking the anti-anxiety meds and to replace them with... can you guess it?... a breathing exercise! She said, "The next time you feel a panic attack coming on, instead of taking the pills, do this simple breathing exercise: pucker your lips like you're about to kiss a fish and breathe in and out through your mouth as long as you can." She emphasized I should breathe normally through the restricted airspace and not slow the breath down nor force the breath out.

Puckering your lips constricts the air flow just enough to give your system the perfect amount of air in and out for the perfect duration. It's basically smoking a cigarette without the cigarette; that's exactly what it would look like. I later found this exercise was also called "Straw Breathing," where you breathe in and out through a straw. It has the same exact effects.

PUT TO THE TEST

To be honest, I wasn't confident that this breathing technique would do much for me, considering I was up to triple my regular dose of the most potent anxiety medication on the market. It was barely doing anything for me, so I didn't believe this breathing technique would do anything either. Then one night in bed, thinking about nothing but sleep, I felt the feeling I feared so much begin to arise. Cortisol and adrenaline began to surge through my body out of nowhere. Slowly, my throat began to close, and my breathing became erratic. My mind went blank. I immediately reached for the bell but realized it was too late and my mother was sleeping. She would never hear it anyway. I grabbed the pill bottle and dumped four pills into the palm of my hand. As I swished saliva around in my mouth, before I could swallow the pills I heard the doctor's voice telling me, "If you continue this, you are on a dark path of no return." That thought scared me even more than the panic attack, because I knew deep down in my soul she was right. If I continued this, I would be a slave to these panic attacks and pills for the rest of my life. I had felt my personal power dwindle as I became more and more dependent on these meds for my survival and integration back into society. I could no longer leave the house without at least five or six pills on me at all times. If I realized I didn't have them, that alone would trigger a panic attack.

In the most desperate manner possible, I closed my eyes, puckered my lips, and began the Straw Breathing exercise the doctor showed me. The entire time, I felt like I was going to die right there on the spot. Then at the very moment (around the third or fourth breath) when I was about to give up (or pass out), something amazing happened... I felt all the anxiety rush out from my body and an overwhelming sense of peace washed over me. I checked my vital signs as my breathing began to normalize and the terror was gone. I put the four pills back onto my night stand and had the most peaceful night's sleep. The next morning I got rid of those pills—and my bell—and never had another panic attack.

You would think this would be the moment when I realized the power of the breath and decided to become a breathwork coach, but nope! I needed to experience more trauma over the course of another decade before I realized the breath is our greatest companion and the most sophisticated divine technology for health and healing.

My experience with the Straw Breathing exercise prompted me to create a breathing tool that facilitates the exercise that saved my life. It's a mini gold (or silver) device in the form of a beautiful pendant that goes around your neck so you can take it everywhere you go. I give them away for free to anyone who enrolls in my Breathwork Detox Program. It's one of the greatest gifts I can give, and I hope the world can benefit from the tools I discovered through my pain, suffering, and ultimate triumph.

When I was having panic attacks and triple-dosing my anti-anxiety meds (before the breath technique), the only reason I was feeling somewhat relieved right away wasn't because of the meds. It was from a mental trigger. Meaning, when I took the meds during a panic attack, the pill didn't even make it into my *stomach* in time to feel relief, nevermind my bloodstream. Any breathing exercise works faster than a pill can. So how could I feel relief if the pill didn't even kick in fast enough? It was from the mental comfort my brain received from the action of swallowing the pill (placebo). This sense of comfort gave my brain permission to begin changing my breathing from sympathetic (stressed) to parasympathetic (relaxed).

When we need to calm down quickly, nothing affects the nervous system faster and more efficiently than the breath. Besides maybe injecting a benzodiazepine directly into your vein (sarcasm), when experiencing the worst type of stress (such as a panic attack), there's only one thing that works immediately for it, and that's conscious breathwork (pranayama). Breathwork is so effective in these situations because changing the pattern of our breathing changes the pattern of information being sent to the brain. How much, how often, and how quickly we inflate our lungs directly affects the brain and how it functions. No food, medication, or exercise acts as quickly as the breath. We can even change our blood PH in just minutes from acid to alkaline, or from alkaline to acid, using certain breathing techniques. This is called "Alkaline Breathing."

KILL THE MONSTERS WHILE THEY'RE SMALL

The best piece of advice I can give you is to *kill the monsters while they're small*. For me, this breathing tool completely eradicated my panic attacks, which were my biggest beasts at the time. Stress and anxiety are separate animals to tame and manage, so they don't grow into bigger monsters you will have to slay later, or be slayed by. I obviously waited way too long and allowed my stress and anxiety to accumulate into panic attacks. The scary part about panic attacks is that you have no warning when they will hit. It's usually random, out of the blue, and when you least expect it.

Unfortunately, we can't predict or avoid trauma, nor do we ask for it, and many times it is not our fault. However, as adults, healing that trauma is indeed our responsibility. If you have any type of stress or anxiety in your life right now, do yourself a giant favor and don't wait as it builds. Do something about it now before anxiety and panic attacks ruin your life and destroy your nervous system.

NERVES, NERVOUSNESS
AND THE NERVOUS SYSTEM

I tried many nootropics (smart drugs and cognitive enhancers) and supplements with the ultimate goal of having more energy and improving my cognitive function. I wasn't aware that what I really wanted was to balance and strengthen my nervous system. That was the secret sauce I was after because the nervous system is what ultimately controls how we feel and react to the world around us.

Our nervous system is crucial to our wellbeing in so many ways, yet people overload their body with stimulants, excessive caffeine, and harmful chemicals that cloud the most crucial operating system. Our brain, spinal cord, and nerves are a communication network that sends and receives signals. Some of these systems are somatic (voluntary) involving skeletal muscular movement. Others are autonomic (involuntary) keeping our system running, heart beating, stomach digesting, and lungs breathing.

There are two parts of the autonomic nervous system that significantly impact your life. The two systems are sympathetic and parasympathetic. Both control the same system but do opposite things. They are antagonistic, meaning that only one of the programs can run at a time. Like love and anger, both operate in the same emotional system, but you can't feel both of these emotions at the same time. It's like how the gas and brake pedals both operate the same machine but don't work at the same time. An example would be inhaling and exhaling. Both operate the lungs, but if you try to inhale and exhale at the same time, you're going to look and feel stupid (and you might pull a lung muscle while trying).

The **sympathetic** division is associated with survival and stress, available to mobilize the body into action. Sympathetic prepares the body for fight or flight by speeding up the heart rate and flooding the system with adrenaline while decreasing digestive activity such as peristalsis. When we feel we're in danger, the body immediately goes into sympathetic division and prepares for action. The major problem of living in "the age of anxiety" is that humanity's default operating system is sympathetic mode. To be constantly running this system can be extremely exhausting for the mind and catastrophic to the body. Besides making us stupid, this is how stress breaks down the body and why it's the root cause of so much illness.

STRESS MAKES YOU STOOPID

Let me explain what I mean by setting the context first. Let's say you are camping in a national park, sipping hot chocolate while roasting marshmallows. Your body would be in parasympathetic mode (rest and digest). If all of a sudden you saw a giant mountain lion 50 feet away and it came charging at you, you would immediately shift into sympathetic mode (fight or flight). All of the energy in your body that was being used to digest your food, detox your system, and produce new healthy cells would temporarily halt and be immediately directed elsewhere for survival. Your heart rate would rapidly increase, and your system would immediately flood with adrenaline. At that moment, all your happy thoughts, creative ideas, and current manifestations would be non-existent. Your body, mind, and all your systems would only give you one of two options to choose from: fight! or flight! If your brain didn't choose either of those two, you would most likely freeze!

Living in the "Age of Anxiety" is just another way of saying that most people walking this earth are constantly stressed. They are stuck in their sympathetic nervous system as their default mode. Just watching the news automatically puts our system into sympathetic mode as well. The problem is that when chemicals and hormones such as epinephrine, adrenaline, and cortisol are constantly being pumped into our system, the body reacts similarly to when the mountain lion is chasing us. Our digestive parastasis slows, causing stagnant chi flow and chronic stomach problems. In addition, all of our creative ideas and vast thinking capabilities shrink and narrow to very primitive life choices. This is how stress makes us stupid! Since the mountain lion (danger) isn't in sight, the brain doesn't know where or when to flee or who to fight, so it constantly feels fear and fights itself. It *looks* for danger rather than reacting to danger. When in fight mode, the sympathetic system also restricts blood vessels, which is the same response we have when we are angry. Living in sympathetic mode can cause us to have chronic anger and unnecessary hostility in our daily life.

For people who don't fight, their natural reaction is the flight response. They are more likely to have anxiety, social withdrawal, or unhealthy addictions. People who have a freeze response are more likely to develop a sloth-like energy when they have goals, visions, and dreams but can't manifest them into reality.

You don't want your default setting to be set on sympathetic. You can practice breathwork to move your mind and body back into homeostasis.

The sympathetic system is connected to mouth breathing, along with all the trauma you've experienced, and all the fight, flight, or freeze moments you've encountered in life. We do the Breathwork Detox via mouth breathing to clear out the cortisol, adrenaline, and stress you've accumulated in your sympathetic nervous system. The breath acts as your interface between mind and body and is the first responder to every situation. It responds to the things we are not yet conscious of. For instance, if someone were to sneak up behind you right now, the first thing you would do is take a giant gasp of air through your mouth to supply your brain with as much oxygen as possible in the shortest amount of time. Then your brain would speed up your breathing to prepare your body to fight or flee. Both of these actions bring the body into its sympathetic nervous system (fight or flight).

When something horrific happens to us, or even when someone is telling us a traumatic story, at the climax of the horror, the first thing we do is take a deep-quick inhale through the mouth. This act locks that fear in the body like a Polaroid camera. Unfortunately, we have a collection of photo albums of negative stored moments that we have accumulated throughout our lifetime. When we breathe in and out through the mouth during Breathwork Detox, we can clear the sympathetic nervous system from trapped and stagnated energies.

Parasympathetic is the opposite of sympathetic. It's rest and relaxation while calming the nervous system. It sends messages to the brain that we are safe. Nose breathing is associated with parasympathetic mode because nose breathing calms and soothes the body. Reduced rate breathing, yoga, and meditation can help the body back into parasympathetic mode and improve sleep, stress levels, and anxiety. Exhaling twice as long than you inhale can help you go to sleep at night. Experiment with seven second exhales, which seems to be the magic number to trigger the body into parasympathetic mode.

NOSE BREATHING VS MOUTH BREATHING

I know, it gets confusing. Before learning about the breath, I would hear various instructors suggest "the golden rule" of breathing in through the nose and out through the mouth. Others say you must breathe in through the nose and out through the nose. Others swear it's best to breathe in through the mouth and out through the nose. I watched other teachers pant like dogs and hiss like lions with their tongues sticking out. Breathwork Detox is best when it's in through the mouth and out through the mouth. Who is right? What is the correct way? Although it's quite confusing to determine the "right or wrong" breathing technique to do in certain situations, there is a golden rule I'll share with you in the simplest terms.

Breathing is your most efficient operating system. For your everyday breathing, breathe in and out as much as you can through the nose. This should be your default mode. It helps your nervous system stay in the parasympathetic system, promoting rest and digestion. Runners, professional athletes, and fighters train using only nasal breathing. Some even tape their mouth closed or wear a mask that lowers their oxygen intake while they train. This is one reason the boxer Floyd Mayweather was so elite at his craft. His stamina was superb. He always maintained closed-mouth nasal breathing for the duration of the fight. You would see his opponent's mouth begin to open, and that was usually the telltale sign that they were fatiguing because their brain and body were requesting more oxygen and prana to continue the bout. Floyd Maywether would move in to dominate his contender with his superb physical conditioning and breath control.

Think of the breath as energy. When you breathe in "energy," you want to breathe up through the nose so that pranic energy reaches the brain before going into the body. Instead of expelling that energy from your mouth, you circulate it back through the nose so you can contain and build more prana. When you breathe in and out through the nose, you maintain a closed circuit.

Since we spend about a third of our lives sleeping, how we breathe while we sleep is important. As someone who suffered from sleep apnea, I learned firsthand how important it is to become conscious of your unconscious breathing patterns. Taping your mouth shut before going to bed is a great way to see if you're nose breathing throughout the night. If you wake up every morning without tape on your mouth, that's a good indication that you may be switching to mouth breathing more frequently than you think. Many people who begin taping before bed notice an improvement in their sleep within just the first few nights by inducing nose breathing.

Breathing through the nose is better because it also senses subtle energies. Hair and mucous membrane tissues line the nose and filter dust and other small particles. It warms or cools and moistens the air you breathe. When you breathe through the nose, it produces more nitrogen oxide which has antibacterial, antiviral, and antifungal properties. Nitric oxide helps lower blood pressure and significantly increases the lungs' oxygen-absorbing capacity, because it is a potent vasodilator and bronchodilator.

Mouth breathing, on the other hand, is associated with the sympathetic nervous system and prepares the body for action. Constantly breathing through the mouth sends a stress response to the body that can fatigue you easily and change your facial structure over time. Studies have recorded the difference in facial development of children who breathe through their mouth compared to those who breathe through their nose.

Mouth breathing is for heavy cleaning and clearing, not everyday breathing. Mouth breathing should NOT be your default mode. Mouth breathing is like driving your hybrid car in gas mode all the time. We only want to use mouth breathing with powerful intention. Breathing through the nose clears the mind, while breathing through the mouth clears the body. Mouth breathing is more emotional and cathartic, because you can't laugh, cry, or sing through the nose.

Breathwork Detox is done completely through the mouth, because mouth breathing is the best way to emotionally detox your system from stress, anxiety, and other harsh energies. When you inhale through the mouth, you are taking in as much oxygen as your body possibly can at one time. When you exhale through the mouth, you are expelling unwanted energy and dumping as much carbon dioxide from your body as fast as you possibly can.

Breathing in and out through the nose is like trying to get a few hundred people out of a room with one tiny door, while mouth breathing is like knocking out the entire wall. Mouth breathing releases everything you don't need from the body: stress, anxiety, emotional pain, and even physical pain. During childbirth using the Lamaze method, new moms are encouraged to breathe through the mouth. Exhaling through the mouth is the expelling force of nature into which a child is born. If mouth breathing is recommended when people are going through the most painful experience in the world, you may want to take notice.

Here's the golden rule to sum it all up: only use mouth breathing for deep cleaning, and breathe through your nose for fine-tuning and maintenance (your default breath).

You can usually determine your dominant nervous system state simply by putting your finger underneath your nostrils and exhaling through your nose. If you feel the flow of your right nostril (*pingala nadi*/yang) more, that means you have increased sympathetic activity. If you feel more air pass through the left nostril (*ida nadi*/yin), this shows a decrease in sympathetic activity and increased parasympathetic. If you have clear breathing through both nostrils equally, this means your nervous system is balanced and your middle channel (*sushumna nadi*) is open and flowing. This is usually only experienced during deep meditation or after the purification process of the nadis in the body. A yogi's main goal in any practice is to increase the supply of prana/chi through the nadis through the Sushmana (the largest main nadi in the center of spine). That will be the only action needed to achieve the bliss and enlightenment they seek. All yogis strive for the perfect state of balance in yin and yang energies.

UPGRADING YOUR PRANA / CHI

The nadis make up our subtle energy body. You can't cut or measure them on anatomical examination because they aren't physical. Western medicine doesn't even acknowledge them; however, they are ESSENTIAL to your health and vitality.

According to Tantric texts, there are approximately 72,000 nadis that house the human body, made up of channels (energetic roads) that create energy highways throughout every fiber of our being. When these pathways and roads are clear, we experience vitality and good health. When these channels become clogged and backed up, we experience either pain, weakness, or disease in the body. The places in the body where these nadis meet create a wheel of energy known as a *Chakra* (a whirling multidimensional center of energy). There are seven main chakras located in the human body, each governing different emotions, senses, and specific areas of life.

One place in the body is considered the capital or "Time Square" of the energetic body where all these pathways and roads intersect. Can you guess where? That's right, the stomach! If traffic is congested at this intersection, every road will be backed up. This is why a Breathwork Detox is so powerful; it's one of the most effective ways of purifying the nadis so you can clear the pathways of your energetic body. It also helps you tap into the power within your energetic core.

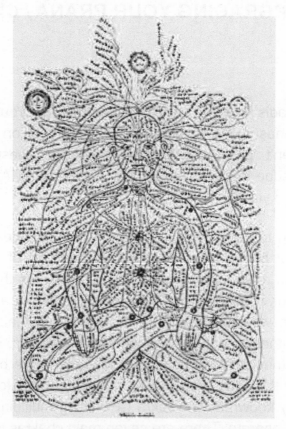

Classic textbook image of the Nadi channels

Understanding what nadis are is so important. The nadis are fascinating, because they house our prana/chi. They power all of our cells with lifeforce energy. They are the energy channels our prana/chi flow through to vitalize our entire being. Some of these channels are wide and rushing, while others are narrow and fine. When our system flows freely, we are vitalized and healthy. When our nadis become clogged or weak, we struggle with mental, emotional, and physical health and clarity.

The quality of your breath is the physical manifestation of the pranic energy flow within your nadi channels. This pranic flow animates us in ways we never fully acknowledge. It regulates our senses and how we perceive the world around us. The energy that runs through your nadis is highly intelligent and very responsive to the world around you. Here's a paragraph from my other bestselling book titled *THE WORLD IS YOURS, The Secrets behind "The Secret,"* which describes an aspect of this intelligence at work:

> Have you ever listened to someone give a speech and they say something that really hits home with you, then suddenly all the hairs on the back of your neck stand straight up? Well, those "goosebumps" that you felt were strong spurts of energy that shot out of the channels of your *Kundalini* called *Nadis*. In other words, when someone is speaking in higher vibrations of truth, and they say something that really resonates with you, your nadis open up and shoot short bursts of energy throughout your body. Yogis refer to this flow of energy as *Prana*. Many people have felt this energy before and experienced those

goosebumps during intense conversations. Whereas energy influxes that are caused from a drastic drop in body temperature are called "Goosebumps," energy influxes caused by spoken words that resonate truth are what I call *"TRUTHBUMPS!"*

On the contrary, have you ever listened to someone give a speech and you can tell that this person is lying or being fraudulent? What you're actually feeling is the low vibrational energies being projected from their energetic field via their vocal cords and your energetic body picks up on that and responds. These lower energetic vibrations felt from lies can be quite uncomfortable to be around, especially to people who are sensitive to energy and have good intuition.

I'm sure you felt this feeling before with a friend or an "Ex." You may have experienced this when confronting this person, as you watched them answer you with a lie—to a question you already knew the answer to. The body never lies and this is why polygraphs (lie detector tests) are so effective. Whenever you lie, unbeknownst to you, your heart rate and blood pressure begin to rise, your breathing becomes faster, your hands start to sweat, and your body temperature begins to change. These kinds of physiological reactions in the body are constantly working and occur in relation to every thought you have.

AWAKENING A SLEEPING GIANT

Hatha yoga and kundalini yoga are practices that help cleanse and purify the nadis and awaken the kundalini within. Kundalini energy itself is "the intelligence" of the nadis system which guides all the unseen energy in your body. Kundalini is the queen of your nervous system and is usually depicted as a "coiled snake" lying dormant at the base of the spine. In Hinduism, kundalini is a form of divine **energy** (or shakti). When awakened and cultivated through breathwork or tantric practice, it is believed to lead to enlightenment.

"In order to get to the crown, you need to conquer the snake."

—Unknown

Egyptian and Hindu deities are all depicted with snakes and cobras around their headdresses, because the deities did the inner work required to raise their kundalini energy from the base of the spine (root chakra) up through their crown chakra. Kundalini is the most powerful energy inside you. Once awakened, it demands respect and requires self-mastery to achieve enlightenment; don't be fooled, this is not child's play. This is a very serious and divine process that should only be attempted if you are 110% committed to the spiritual path and journey of purification.

Kundalini has only one intention: to purify your energy for spiritual liberation and enlightenment. No greater achievement in life is more rewarding than purifying your nadis and mastering your kundalini energy. This is the liberation we all seek. The only caveat to awakening your kundalini is that it's so powerful it has the potential to open a Pandora's box. If you have a lot of trauma and aren't willing to continue the inner work and create a solid practice to clear it all out (start to finish), you may not want to blow open the lid to your volcano. Once you awaken the sleeping giant and this energy is activated, it's nearly impossible to put it back to sleep and live a normal life again. Some people activate this energy in one breathwork session or kundalini class and immediately become enlightened and feel the indefinite feelings of joy and bliss for the rest of their life, but most people have a better chance of being struck by lightning.

Many yogi traditions believe kundalini is a unifying cosmic energy synonymous with God energy and sexual energy. Since both God energy and sexual energy have the power to create life itself, there is no greater or more powerful energy available in the body than kundalini energy. Kundalini lies dormant in many people, no matter how smart, rich, or poor they are. Because they aren't ready for the purification process, that energy won't awaken. I mention kundalini energy in this book because when my students are doing breathwork, many of them begin activating their kundalini energy. Their body will begin to shake or their head will stretch back into yoga poses, all of which are common during breathwork. Their body is moving stagnant energy up and down the spine, ridding it of any spiritual sludge or toxins that impede their energy flow, vitality, and higher states of consciousness. Activated by the breath, the kundalini is the intelligence responsible for moving these energies out of the body to take the student to the next level of their personal and spiritual evolution.

THE POWER OF THE CHI

hen the kundalini is awakened and the nadis are clear and flowing properly, you will experience an increase in lightness in the body, almost feeling weightless. You will feel this vast, boundless awareness all around you, as if you are floating through life. As Swami Sivananda says in his book *The Science of Pranayama*, when the nadis are purified there is a "lightness of the body, brilliancy in complexion, increase of the gastric fire, leanness of the body, and the absence of restlessness." He also states, "In the first stage purification perspiration arises without effort, the middle stage is the tremor of the body, and the last stage is levitation in the air" (meaning liberation, nirvana, and euphoria).

This next story I am about to share is something I was going to leave out of the book, but since you are reading this, I must have decided to keep it in. It's one thing to read about the power of chi and prana and try to imagine there must be some truth in what these yogis and gurus are saying; it's entirely different to experience it for yourself.

I had been experimenting with intermittent fasting and was surprised by how well my body responded and how toned my muscles were getting with very little food and nutrition in my system. I distinctly remember looking at my body and examining my arm and legs, noticing how big my muscles were getting. I felt and looked strong; it was incredible!

Then Thanksgiving rolled around, and for two days, and two days only, I began eating badly. Even my energy felt off. By the end of the second day, I looked at my body. My legs and arms were skinny and untoned. It was as if I was looking at a completely different body; just two days ago, I was much larger and more built. The fact that I ate more food and became skinnier in such a short amount of time made no sense to me. Then, the very next day, I remember feeling a very slight pain around my heart and back area, then suddenly a cooling sensation rushed through my body like ice in my veins. It felt great! As this was happening, I felt a sense of vitality and energy course through my body. As this energy made its way through me, I could immediately feel my emotional state lifting, my awareness and mental clarity enhancing, and even my posture was shifting. I felt lighter and more buoyant. I looked in the mirror and noticed my eyes were more blue and my complexion was more clear. I got a phone call shortly after. During the call, I noticed my breathing was stronger and my voice had noticeably changed. It sounded slightly deeper than normal, and it felt as if my words were just flowing. Later that night, I noticed my muscle tonality and physique had morphed back to what it was a few days ago. The insanity of this experience is that it all happened in just minutes or possibly even seconds.

CLEARING THE PATH!

I decided to share this experience because it happened to me several times afterward. I now know this is the purification process of the nadis that the yogis spoke of, and the trembling and torturous feeling I had felt in my body over the years was from all the energetic blockages I had which made this process difficult. It wasn't until I discovered breathwork that I was able to bust through these blockages and begin to see the light at the end of the tunnel. The breath was the secret sauce.

The practice called "Alternate Nostril Breathing" is highly effective in clearing your nadis and balancing your sympathetic and parasympathetic systems. While blocking the right nostril with your thumb, deeply and slowly breathe up the left nostril. This stimulates the creative right brain, your emotional side, which is also associated with lunar energy, femine energy, and yin energy (this is that ice-cold energy I felt running through me when I had my first breakthrough). Before exhaling, block your left nostril with the ring finger on the same hand and exhale through the right nostril deeply and slowly. When all the air is out, inhale through the same nostril deeply and slowly. This stimulates the logical and rational left brain associated with male energy, sun/ fire energy, and yang energy (the opposite of what I felt).

When doing this technique, I like to repeat the mantra, "Love wisdom and power-balancing every hour...Love wisdom and power-balancing every hour... Love wisdom and power-balancing every hour..." Doing this practice for just three to five minutes a day will balance the left and right hemispheres of the brain. This is highly effective in grounding the mind and balancing the nervous system. Some yogis say if you have become disciplined in your spiritual practice with a pure mind, doing this exercise every day for three months will completely clear your nadis.

How do you know when your nadis are purified? When you monitor the quality of your thoughts and actions, you will see a direct reflection of how purified your nadis are. I believe pranayama and breathwork are some of the fastest, most natural ways to clear these channels. Doing breathwork first, then three to five minutes of alternate nostril breathing is the perfect breathwork combination to clear and balance the nervous system.

GET "OFF" MY NERVES

Have you ever heard someone say, "That person gets on my nerves?" The funny thing is, that's exactly what happens. When we have an issue with someone, that conflict shows up in our energy field. Somewhere in the body in the nadi channels, an impediment of energy manifests. This disharmony can literally cause discomfort, and you will be emotionally impacted. Hence, "That person gets on my nerves." When that person comes around or their name comes up, you will be triggered. Similar to how muscle memory occurs in the body, or how neural-pathways are created in the brain, there is an energetic pathway created in your energy field when you interact with certain people, triggering certain feelings or emotions. If something hasn't been resolved, you will feel uneasy or irritated just by thinking of them.

> *"Holding onto anger is like drinking poison and expecting the other person to die."*
>
> —Buddha

The practice of breathwork is so powerful. With the breath, you can clear your energy field of any anger or resentment clogging these energy channels/meridians (nadis). When you do the work to clear that energy out, you are able to truly move on. If not, you're only hurting yourself, because the way you feel has nothing to do with the other person and everything to do about you, your spiritual evolution, and emotional maturity.

Ask yourself: Do the emotions of anger, hate, or resentment feel good in my body? Of course not, they feel horrible. So let me ask you another question: When you hold onto grudges, anger, hate, or resentment, who feels that energy... you or the other person? You do! In fact, they don't feel any of it, and subconsciously that will upset you even more because you're still hurt by what they supposedly did. The problem is we collect so many of these grudges that we forget we're even holding onto them, so we start storing them. The body knows it needs to purge toxic energy one way or another; if breathwork or other inner work isn't done, the body will project that anger into the world, and to people who usually don't deserve it, like your parents, your partner, your friend, or your children. All they need to do to trigger you is to breathe on a wound that you buried, and you lash out. The root cause of this reactive behavior occurs unbeknownst to you. After all, people tend to forget where and why they store things, just like they forget where they put their keys or last summer's sunglasses.

Implementing the practice of breathwork *will* definitely bring up something real that you need to heal. However, not everything needs to be brought to your consciousness to heal from it. The breath can clear things that were insignificant but were buried under so much other stuff. This is how massive breakthroughs happen, and why many people experience a landslide avalanche of energy clearing and healing occurring all at once during breathwork.

When events like this happen, everything can shift and change in an instant. Your behavior changes and how you react to life changes as well. You will find yourself becoming more centered, at peace, and making better choices every day. The minute and trivial choices we make ultimately change our relationships and shape our destiny. Breathwork has the power to transform you from the inside out, and your self-transformation can make a bigger impact on everything and everyone around you. This is hard to grasp and imagine, yet every great teacher who has walked the path stated, "Being the change we wish to see is how we change the world."

THE HEROES

"If you want to awaken all of humanity, then awaken all of yourself. If you want to eliminate the suffering in the world, then eliminate all that is dark and negative in yourself. Truly, the greatest gift you have to give is that of your own self-transformation."

—Lao Tzu

The heroic energies of forgiveness and compassion will save humanity. You may be thinking, what about love? I believe love is not a singular emotion; rather, love is the foundational ingredient in every human emotion. Some emotions have more of it, and others much less. Joy is simply the union of love and happiness. Compassion is the combination of love and understanding. When the ingredient of love is at its highest capacity, it is called unconditional love. When the ingredient of love is at its lowest, it is hate. However, hate is not an organic emotion; hate simply occurs when love is not present. All negative emotions are the absence of its fundamental ingredient: love.

LIGHT IT UP

"The people that are trying to make the world worse never take a day off, why should I? Light up the darkness."

—Bob Marley

The only way to transmute negative feelings into positive emotions is through the actions of love: compassion and forgiveness. They say forgiveness is the most selfish thing in the world, because it's the greatest thing you can do for yourself. Holding onto anger, resentment, hate, jealousy, and simple grudges allows them to become residents in the space where love once lived. These energies block out love, becoming toxic to the soul, because they don't just block out love for others, but also love for oneself. Therefore we *must* forgive to release this poison and evict these unwanted guests.

Forgiveness is a gift that we give ourselves, because we can only love ourselves as much as we forgive ourselves. All forgiveness is ultimately self-forgiveness, an act of self-love.

If we feel someone hurt us or broke our heart, we must understand they didn't literally break our heart. There are no x-rays of a broken heart. What they broke was our expectations, and as we know, expectations lead to disappointment. Therefore, we must forgive that person for NOT being who we "expected" them to be; then we must forgive ourselves for "expecting" that person to be anything other than who they are. Acceptance is an act of compassion: the expression of love and understanding. We can never change or fix what's broken inside someone else, and they can never fix what's broken inside us. We can only offer a safe space for someone to accept themselves to allow them to heal at their own pace. This is the definition of "holding space" that you often hear amongst various healing modalities. Even if this person hurt us dearly, in the grander scheme of human evolution, they helped us understand ourselves and define our morals. That helped us grow stronger and become a better person to make better decisions. Ultimately this person didn't come to harm you; they came to serve you!

If forgiveness is the only way to release ourselves from these shackles of the past, then HOW do we forgive? It's easy to say "Just forgive them and let it go," or "Just forgive yourself and love yourself." But seriously, how do we do that?

The golden key to transmuting negative emotions into positivity is practicing the art of *perception*. The power of perception is the greatest way to forgive. When we change our perception, we automatically change our thoughts and emotions towards that person and situation. We can only control our perspective and attitude in life—not life itself, nor the events that play out. As Wayne Dyer said, "When we change the way we look at things, the things we look at change." We cannot control what someone did to us, but we can control how we *perceive* what they did to us. The only way to change things is to change our perception. Realistically we cannot change past situations and events at all;

things that have happened are in the past for a reason. What we *can* change is ourselves as we reframe how we view what happened in the past. Perception is our superpower.

"We don't see things as they are, we see them as we are."

—Anaïs Nin

I use a very powerful process for forgiveness and self-realization, the combination of breathwork and journaling. I tried many modalities and this combo seems to be the most effective and transformative. I began sharing the process with my mother. It became so transformative for both of us that we developed a program called *Self Talk Therapy*, a new mental health modality that has the singular power to change the world. It's also the missing integration piece to all breathwork practices.

In teaching breathwork over the years, the only challenge I could identify was integration. Breathwork is so powerful and transformative that it's almost *too* powerful and transformative. When you begin to practice breathwork and "clean house," you stir up the stuff that's been holding you back (which is the whole point). The issue is that many people don't know how to deal with everything that comes *after* breathwork. They come to a breathwork event, get their world rocked, their kundalini activated, and their third eye blasted open, only to go home thinking, "WTF just happened to me?" Many times, I had to ground and reintegrate people back onto this planet after breathwork, because they underestimated its power, which is ultimately their own healing power. Unfortunately, there are not many support groups or tools given to people after breathwork to help them process and integrate the work they just did or to manage the massive healing that took place for them. Visit SelfTalkTherapy. com if you wish to become certified in teaching this modality, or if you simply want to learn how to use it for your own transformation.

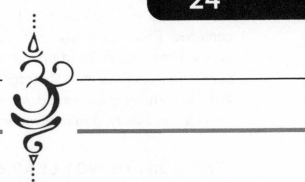

WHY MAKE BREATHWORK
A DAILY PRACTICE?

Breathwork reduces your blood pressure, heart rate, carbon dioxide, and the stress hormone cortisol by 20%. It also increases your oxygen, dopamine and serotonin levels while helping regulate your immune system. In a nutshell, breathwork reduces all the things we don't want in life (toxic waste), while simultaneously increasing the things we all strive for (improved mood and health). Breathwork not only improves concentration and induces clearer thinking, it cleanses stagnant energy and brings calmness to the nervous system and mastery over emotions. What more can we ask for from a practice?

The number one beverages in the world are coffee and energy drinks, yet breathwork boosts energy levels and stamina naturally without the jitters. Breathwork boosts every system in your body and circulates your prana/chi, which helps you look and feel more vibrant, present, and centered. Either way, wouldn't it be nice to clear out all the junk you've accumulated in your life and fill that space with pure love, gratitude, and life force energy just by breathing? What dreams or goals would you start knocking out with this new clarity, vitality, and motivation?

THE COST OF NOT LEARNING BREATHWORK

When I started doing breathwork daily, it wasn't because I wanted to; it was because I felt so darn guilty when I didn't, because I knew how good it made me feel when I did. Every time I would slack and skip a week or two, I could noticeably tell the difference in my daily life. Breathwork became an outlet for me that allowed me to manage all the stresses of the world and helped me connect to a higher intelligence that guides me through life.

The cost of not making breathwork a daily practice is a price I'm not willing to pay. If I had to choose only one modality or practice for my overall health and well-being, such as prayer, pranayama, meditation, gym, exercise, cardio, or yoga, I would do breathwork, hands down. I know this may seem like a biased statement, and it is, but after becoming certified in life coaching, meditation, hypnotherapy, NLP, reiki mastery, and fitness training, I learned breathwork is the secret sauce. Breathwork is <u>all the above combined</u> and gives me the best physical, mental, and emotional feeling afterward. People work out physically and eat healthy for one reason: to feel good energetically and emotionally. Breathwork reverse engineers that process by allowing you to work out energetically so you feel good physically.

Many people begin a yoga practice to help them heal from an injury or to become more flexible. Although this may be what gets them into yoga, it's not the reason everyone stays. True yoga isn't about flexibility; it's about stilling the mind and gaining control over the body through the breath *while in the yoga pose.* Actually, the breath and mind-body connection is what every yogi strives to master during yoga. If just being still brought enlightenment, every lazy person would be enlightened, but they're not. If complete mastery over the body brought enlightenment, then professional body-builders would become dalai lamas, but they don't. If just being flexible brought enlightenment, then all contortionists and gymnasts would be spiritual masters, but they're not. The communion of mind, body, and spirit, in unison with the breath and strong intention, is the force that magnetizes us toward enlightenment.

Don't get me wrong. I love and practice yoga and meditation daily, but breathwork is the secret sauce and the one modality I can't live without. Although I teach breathwork to students around the world, the truth is I need this practice just as much as they do. I didn't discover this modality in deep meditation or in an ayahuasca ceremony, nor did it drop in my mind as I was hiking up a mountain on a spiritual expedition in the Himalayas. I found this modality through my journey of pain and suffering. Many people refer to me as a breath teacher and expert, but in reality I am a student of the breath as much as I am a teacher. Breathwork continues to teach me so much about myself and life and I'm honored to show people how they can tap into this power for themselves.

WHERE TO GO FROM HERE

When should you start? As they say, one day or day one? The choice is yours! We all procrastinate, but if you want your life to change, you have to change your life! It's that simple! Procrastination is like masturbation; in the end, we just end up screwing ourselves! Since old ways don't open new doors, we can't expect new results if we're not willing to try new things. The Universe won't do anything for you, but it will meet you halfway. All you need to do is SHOW UP! 80% of all success in life is just showing up; the other 20% is giving your 100% when you do. Know that someone, somewhere, is counting on you to be the best version of yourself. It may be your spouse, your friend, or your child. It could even be your future child or your future soulmate who is waiting for you to get your life together before you meet them. If you can't show up for yourself, then at least you can show up for them.

If something needs to change in your life, chances are that something is YOU. Life doesn't have a remote control; you have to get off your butt and make the changes. <u>Committing</u> to developing a breathwork practice is the single most powerful thing you can do after reading this book. Remember, indecision *is* a decision. If you wait, you miss out on the most powerful force and greatest ally to change: momentum! The moment you make a decision, something phenomenal happens and the Universe begins clearing the path of change for you.

> *"Begin at once to live, and count each separate day as a separate life."*
>
> —Seneca

Breathwork is the very first thing I do when I wake up in the morning because it sets the tone for my entire day. "If you win the morning, you win the day," says author and entrepreneur Tim Ferriss. A morning routine forms the foundation you need to build anything of value in life. If your foundation is weak, whatever you build will eventually crumble. Your morning routine is a building block. Once you set it in place, you should never move it. Your morning routine shapes the habits which determine your destiny and ultimately create who you become. These building blocks are non-negotiable; you must do them every day to achieve your desired outcome. This is a firm negotiation with your higher-self, your future self. Keep these blocks in place so you can build on them and be productive.

FINAL WORDS

None of us wants to live a stressed-out life with anxiety or depression. We all want to be happy, but we need to know how. Harvard University is one of the oldest and most prestigious highly-respected schools in the nation. It was founded well before America gained its independence. Harvard has had many brilliant professors and amazing courses throughout its years, but its most popular course of all time was a positive psychology class called "The Secret to Living a Happy Life," conducted by Professor Tal Ben-Shahar. The one thing we all seek the most from life is intangible: happiness.

Maybe you're doing fine and just need a boost, or maybe you feel you've hit rock bottom. If so, just know that rock bottom is a good place to be, because you get to see your roots and who you are. Plus, there's only one way to go from rock bottom, and that's up! I know life may be challenging, but if you feel your path has been difficult, it's simply because your calling is much higher. Remember, God gives His toughest battles to his strongest soldiers. These experiences qualify you, because they give you more empathy and compassion for others as you help them through their hardships. You have been chosen, not forgotten. Your struggles are not your punishment; they're your training.

> *"Grapes must be crushed to make wine. Diamonds form under pressure. Olives are pressed to release oil. Seeds grow in darkness. Whenever you feel crushed, under pressure, pressed, or in darkness, you're in a powerful place of transformation and transmutation. Trust the process."*
> —Lalah Delia

From now on, be grateful for everything you've endured and experienced in life, for those experiences made you who you are and who you will soon become. Now it's your job to turn your pain into power, and your wounds into wisdom. It's your duty to take your mess and turn it into your message, so you can switch from being the victim into the victor. This is how you turn your traumas into trophies and reap the benefits you've already earned.

When you make these decisions and embrace vulnerability, the Universe then gives you the opportunity to turn your adversity into prosperity by helping others own their struggles and hardships as well. The thing about vulnerability and things like guilt, shame and regret, is that no one wants to talk about them, but the less you want to talk about these things, the more you have them.

> *"If you don't have any shadows, you're not standing in the light."*
> —Stefani Joanne Angelina Germanotta

My mother once told me, "The dark is beautiful; it's evil that we're fighting." The dark is just as beautiful as the light. Without it, neither would be defined, nor would we see their individual beauty. Without darkness, sleep would be impossible, the stars wouldn't shine, and the seeds wouldn't grow. Therefore, you must accept your light and accept what you perceive to be darkness. Both are gifts that make up who you've become.

> *"Our deepest fear is not that we are inadequate. Our deepest fear is that we are powerful beyond measure. It is our light, not our darkness that most frightens us."*
> —Marianne Williamson

Own your life and embrace what you perceive to be your weaknesses and don't worry about being judged, because no one can hold anything against you that you've accepted about yourself. There is tremendous power in vulnerability. When you own your insecurities and wear them like armor, they become your confidence and no one can hurt you ever again.

You now have all the tools you need to equip you on your journey. A new chapter has begun, and you can create any beginning you wish. Remember, it's never too late to start investing in yourself and begin working on your dream. Right now, in this very moment, you are the youngest you will be for the rest of your life, so take full advantage! Now *Breathe*, and remember who you are and what you came here to do, because the time is now!

THE ~~END~~ BEGINNING

Personal Request: If you could please post a short review of this book on Amazon.com for me, I would greatly appreciate it. Also, please tag me and share this book on your social media pages (@ManFromTheStars) and recommend this book to friends and family who suffer from excess stress or anxiety and would benefit from the tools in this book.

P.S. Be sure to scan the image below because I look forward to breathing with you and your friends. See you at my next Breathwork Detox event! :)

Text BREATHE to 76626

RESOURCES:

To watch a video of me showing you "How to Do Breathwork," along with suggestions on "Before Breathwork TIPS" and "After Breathwork TIPS," plus a Bonus video on "Grounding exercises," you can either join me in my next Breathwork Detox online adventure found here: https://linktr.ee/manfromthestars, or you can enroll in my Breathwork Detox program at www.BreathworkDetox.com, where I give you all the tools you'll need to start a powerful Breathwork Detox practice at home and begin transforming your life from the inside out.

Below is a list of some modalities and habits I have compiled over the past ten years. This is not a list of everything I've tried. Rather, this is a list of everything that seemed to work for me and made an impact on my overall health and well-being. Most of this was trial and error. I'm leaving out everything that did not work for me. I emphasize "for me" because everyone is different and what worked for me may not work for you, and vice versa.

- 20-30 mins of Breathwork Detox per day
- 3-5 mins alternate nostril breathing afterward

- Cut out coffee or switch to decaf
- Cup of peppermint tea and journal for 5 minutes (Self-Talk Therapy)
- A minimum 20 mins of movement (exercise) in the morning.
- Do a heavy workout at least once a week or twice a month to strengthen the nervous system.
- Open up the body by stretching or doing some form of yoga.
- Drink lots of water, more than you think you should drink.
- 3-10 minute cold showers in the morning
- Get in nature. Take shoes off and ground yourself to the earth.
- Eat clean and be intuitive (try to cut out all sugar, red meat, or too many carbs)
- Epsom salt bath at night (1-3 times per week)
- Communicate to your Creator (pray)
- Listen to your Creator (meditate)

OTHER MODALITIES THAT HELPED MY NERVOUS SYSTEM HEAL:

- Acupuncture
- Chiropractor
- Tummy massages (page 29)
- Chinese herbs that move stagnant chi in the spleen and stomach (you may need a prescription from a Chinese medical practitioner)
- Essential oils: I use Young Living Oils. Members receive 24% off (Member number: 1657376)

LIFE TIPS WITH BOOK RECOMMENDATIONS:

- Life Pillars to live by... (read *The Four Agreements: A Practical Guide to Personal Freedom* by Don Miguel Ruiz)
- AWAKEN your hidden powers and learn the Laws of The Universe... (read *The World is Yours, The Awakening—The Secrets Behind "The Secret"* by Kurtis Lee Thomas)
- Practice being wrong even when you're right... (read *How to Win Friends and Influence People* by Dale Carnegie)
- Practice manifesting confidence, then practice manifesting money (read *Think and Grow Rich* by Napoleon Hill)

THE WORLD IS (Y)OURS
THE AWAKENING
THE SECRETS BEHIND "THE SECRET"
KURTIS LEE THOMAS

TABLE OF CONTENTS

Their "Time" Has Come To An End
Experiencing Different Dimensions
Making This New Dimension A Reality

CHAPTER 16
Ascension-What is it exactly?
How To Ascend
The Final Battle
Who Will Survive Armageddon? (The Ascension Roster)
It's Already Happening, And Here's How
You're Not Going Crazy (Ascension Symptoms)
Our Bodies Are Changing Before Our Eyes
Why Now? Why Us?
Planet Earth is ALIVE
Law of Relativity
No Need To Worry
How Will We Know This Is Happening?
When Will All This Happen?

CHAPTER 17
THE EVENTS
How Should I Prepare?
Who Should I Believe?
Google: Your New Best Friend

CHAPTER 18
The Best Advice Ever Given To Man
United We Stand, Divided We Fall
Law of Correspondence
We Are Who We Have Been Looking For
We Have Everything We Need

CHAPTER 19
It's (y)Our Time
Choosing Your 'Perception Lenses'
Final Words
Remember To Remember
The Beginning

Made in the USA
Monee, IL
09 January 2021

56986757R00111